Corporate Dynamism

Corporate Dynamism

How world class companies became world class

Cuno Pümpin

Gower

© 1989 by ECON Executive, ECON Verlags GmbH, Düsseldorf, Wien, New York

Originally published in 1989 in German as Das Dynamik-Prinzip by ECON Executive, ECON Verlags GmbH, Düsseldorf, Wien, New York

Published in 1991 by
Gower Publishing Company Limited
Gower House
Croft Road
Aldershot
Hants GU11 3HR
England

Gower Publishing Company
Old Post Road
Brookfield
Vermont 05036
USA

British Library Cataloguing in Publication Data

Pümpin, Cuno
    Corporate Dynamism
    1. Business enterprise. Success
    I. Title
    650.1

Library of Congress Cataloging-in-Publication Data

Pümpin, Cuno
    Corporate dynamism: how world-class companies became world-class/Cuno Pümpin
      p. cm.
    Includes bibliographical references and index.
    1. Organizational change. 2. Organizational change--Case studies. 3. Organizational effectiveness. 4. Organizational effectiveness--Case studies. I. Title
HD58.8.P86 1991
338.7'4--do20

            91-9172
            CIP

Translated from the German by Katie Lewis

ISBN 0 566 07277 7
Printed and bound in Great Britain by
Billing and Sons Limited, Worcester.

Contents

Preface

How this book came into being

The idea of writing this book developed during a research seminar which I was running together with the Tom Peters Group not far from London. Our group of thirty leading managers was asked what problems companies would have to solve in the coming years, with a view to the impending millennium. One of the key points to emerge was that companies would have to find new ways of being dynamic. The concept presented here has moved some way away from our first conclusions at that time and from the formulas which Tom Peters evolved.

Around the same time I found myself working on the theory of corporate dynamism in practice, when I was responsible for a company which was operating at a loss, so that every day's delay took it further into the red. This situation called for dynamic, rapid change in order to reverse the downward trend.

The third and final spur to writing the book was the turbulence of the business world today, shaken by fluctuating exchange rates, the stock market crash of 1987, quantum leaps in technology, new social trends and in particular the movement towards political integration (Europe 1992). In such a climate the only way to succeed is to adapt, and that means being flexible and dynamic.

In presenting my material I originally intended to follow the time-honoured scheme of strategy, structure and so on, but this would have made it difficult to look at things from a new angle. I have therefore chosen a more unconventional and stimulating scheme, and have focused on the management of value potential and multiplication, neither of which have so far received much attention. I am of course aware that this incurs the risk, as every innovation does, that the gap between the familiar and the new will be too great. But it seems to me that we have to overturn the patterns of thought which have become established over the last two decades, and that this may be a sensible way to do it. I am sure that in the future there will be further, important steps in this direction.

The sources of this book are manifold. My projects with Tom Peters and Michael Porter form a valuable foundation. Then come my personal experiences as management consultant to internationally active firms. Most important of all are the many interviews my colleagues and I have held with leading European entrepreneurs who, according to our criteria, are particularly 'dynamic'. Finally, my frequent discussions with colleagues and friends have been indispensable and, like the existing literature on the subject, have contributed greatly to the conclusions presented here.

My research methods were largely casuistic. Together with my colleagues I selected eighteen European companies which were going through particularly dynamic phases. We used a number of criteria. Principally the companies had to have increased benefits for their stakeholders several times over within a fairly short time. We obviously required access to a lot of information, and relied heavily on secondary material such as Annual Reports, magazine articles, corporate brochures, company histories and so on. We also stipulated that we should be able to hold extensive interviews with senior representatives of the company concerned. Finally we did not want to restrict ourselves to one country, and have drawn our analyses from the whole of Western Europe as well as referring to some American and Japanese companies.

Admittedly I cannot claim that the selection of companies is truly representative. Also the analyses were necessarily undertaken retrospectively, so that we were not aiming to predict the future development and success or otherwise of the companies concerned. These case studies serve as models to check our hypotheses against real events. In practice this meant that some of the hypotheses we developed at the beginning of the research process were revised as we carried out our analysis. Two of the cornerstones of my new concept – value potential and multiplication – only crystallized fully in the course of our research.

Acknowledgements

I am delighted to have this opportunity to express my most sincere gratitude to all the entrepreneurs named below for the frank and very interesting interviews with which they contributed to the development of this book. Their examples are worthy of imitation in many respects.

ASEA AB, Västeras (Dr Curt Nicolin, President); Bank in Liechtenstein, Vaduz (Christian Norgren, former Chairman of the Board); Bertelsmann AG, Gütersloh (Dr Marc Wössner, President); Cartier SA, Paris (Pierre

Haquet, Executive Vice President and Michel Gutin, Executive Vice President); Club Méditerranée SA, Paris (Gilbert Trigano, President and Chief Executive Officer; Thierry Piekar, Vice President); Crossair AG, Basle (Moritz Suter, Chief Executive Officer); Electrolux AB, Stockholm (Hans Werthén, Chairman of the Board); Forbo AG, Zurich (Dr R. Ruepp, Chief Executive Officer); Glaxo plc, London (Sir Paul Girolami, Chairman of the Board); Hanson plc, London (M. G. Taylor, Vice-Chairman of the Board; Alexander C. Notter, Vice President); IKEA, Älmhult (Ingvar Kamprad, Founder); Jacobs Suchard AG, Zurich (Klaus Jacobs, Chairman of the Board); Metro International AG, Zug (Hans-Dieter Cleven, Member of the Board and Executive Vice President; Erwin Conradi, Member of the Board and Chief Executive Officer; Dr Hannjörg Hereth, Member of the Board and Executive Vice President); Mikron AG, Biel (Dr Theo Fässler, Chairman of the Board); Nokia Corporation, Helsinki (Kari Kairamo, former President); Ing. C. Olivetti & C., S.p.A., Ivrea (Dr Bruno Lamborghini, Vice President); Sarna AG, Sarnen (Dr H. P. Käser, Executive Vice President); Schweizerische Kreditanstalt, Zurich (Robert Jeker, President).

In the mid-1980s I had the opportunity to talk to some senior representatives of Japanese companies about changes of structure and dynamic adaptation to new developments. These discussions also had an important influence on the present work, and I would like to thank these individuals.

Very special thanks are due to various people with whom I have been able to discuss my theory of corporate dynamism in detail. I should like to mention here Dr Markus Altwegg, Member of Executive Committee, F. Hoffmann-La Roche & Co. AG, Basle; Professor Knut Bleicher, University of St Gall; Professor Silvio Borner, University of Basle; Professor E. Brauchlin, University of St Gall; Max Burger-Calderon, Partner, MMG Patricof & Co. AG, Zollikon; Walter Ernst, Vice President, Allgemeine Treuhand AG (ATAG), Zurich; Professor Peter Gomez, University of St Gall; Dr Carlo Imboden, Chief Executive Officer, Implementa AG, Berne; James A. Kohlberg, Partner, Kohlberg & Co., New York; Alex O. Lendi, Member of the Executive Committee, Hilti AG, Schaan; Dr Peider Mengiardi, Chairman of the Board, Allgemeine Treuhand AG (ATAG), Basle; Jeffrey D. Tannenbaum, Vice President, Kohlberg & Co., New York; G. Richard Thoman, President and Chief Executive Officer, American Express International Corporation, New York; Dr Hans von Werra, President, Sprecher & Schuh Holding AG, Aarau; Professor Dr Hans Peter Wehrli, University of Zurich; Dr Hans Widmer, Chairman of the Board, Schweiter AG, Horgen; Dr Hans A. Wüthrich, Partner, D&RSW AG, Zurich.

I would like to thank my academic colleagues, Toni Calabretti, Balz Ryf and Michele Vela. They have not only carried out the many basic tasks involved with the publication of any book, but have also stimulated me in many critical discussions with their impartiality and creativity. Thanks are due as well to my secretary, Mrs Eschmann, who has carried out many administrative tasks with great energy.

I also owe a great debt to Mrs Katie Lewis, who was responsible for the translation of my German manuscript into English. This book came into being through her considerable effort and knowledgeable work.

My most especial thanks, finally, to my wife Ruth and my daughters Simone, Catherine and Susanne, who have always supported my work with great understanding and made sure that I could carry on undisturbed.

During my first ten years as Extraordinarius at the University of St Gall, between 1974 and 1984, I was lucky enough to work with four personal assistants: Günther Pipp, Hans O. Henkell, Walter Stecher and Hans A. Wüthrich (in chronological order). Since the beginning of their professional lives they have all achieved considerable success, and it fills me with particular pride that all four have since become independent, dynamic entrepreneurs. This book is dedicated to them.

Cuno Pümpin
Jona, April 1990

Prologue

Two success stories

Electrolux: From small vacuum cleaner manufacturer to Number One in white goods

About 20 years ago the market for white goods (refrigerators, freezers, washing machines, cookers, etc.) was defined by national boundaries. In every country there was a fight between several suppliers all wanting a bigger market share. In West Germany, for example, the main competitors were AEG, Bauknecht, Bosch, Miele and Siemens. Many national markets were already approaching saturation point.

At that time Electrolux was known principally as a Swedish vacuum cleaner manufacturer which also produced and supplied refrigerators on a small scale in the Swedish market. Its turnover in 1967 was 850m. DM, much lower than that of the international market leaders in white goods.

By 1988 the picture was as follows: Electrolux is the largest manufacturer of white goods in the world, with a total turnover of 22,000m. DM. Many of the stakeholders in Electrolux have profited from this expansion. Customers enjoy improved quality and lower prices. Electrolux now has 140,500 employees compared with 19,150 in 1967 and provides new, interesting, challenges for many capable young managers. Investors have also benefited. Share prices rose (after adjustment) from 23 SKr. at the end of 1967 to over 310 SKr. at the beginning of 1989. The state has profited from Electrolux in that the tax revenue of 22.8m. SKr. in 1967 rose to 914m. SKr. in 1987. Finally, suppliers have gained orders because of the growth of the company and have not experienced problems with Electrolux like those of some other companies (for instance in 1982

Bauknecht went bankrupt and AEG came close to bankruptcy). Overall, in the last twenty years Electrolux has provided significantly greater benefits for all its stakeholders, that is, for all the organizations and people who have dealings with it, than comparable competitors.

How has Electrolux developed so fast?

In 1967 the Swedish industrialist and chief shareholder of Electrolux, Marcus Wallenberg, appointed 47-year-old Hans Werthén as head of Electrolux, which at that time was stagnating. Werthén saw that conventional marketing strategy would make little difference in the virtually saturated white goods market. Trying to win a larger market share by aggressive sales tactics would have involved the company in costly advertising and price wars and achieved marginal advances at best.

Werthén wanted to take the company into new dimensions. He predicted that more and more medium-sized white goods manufacturers in Europe would get into difficulties, and saw in this a great opportunity for his own company: taking over such firms and restructuring them could be very profitable, though perhaps less in the marketplace than on the financial and production side.

In fact, on the financial side Werthén was often able to dispose of surplus assets after the takeovers and in this way recover more than the purchase price. Unit costs were significantly reduced by merging production, which led to a clear improvement on margins vis-à-vis the competition. The international exchange of production expertise made improvements in quality possible, which was good for the customers.

His strategy centred firmly on the acquisition and restructuring of white goods companies, as shown in Figure P.1. 'I learnt from the Habsburgs, who increased their empire by marriage,' says Werthén.[1]

In contrast most German (and European) competitors such as AEG and Bauknecht concentrated on improving their marketing mix. For example, AEG invested heavily in product design, and its machines often won awards. But events have shown very clearly that in largely saturated markets simply optimizing marketing activities is not the answer. Many white goods manufacturers who followed this route (AEG, Bauknecht, Zanussi) have ended up on the verge of bankruptcy, or even toppled over it. Many other businesses were bought at the last minute by Electrolux, and brought back to good health through its restructuring strategy.

To establish a strategy of acquisition and restructuring is one thing: to carry it through is another. Here Electrolux has been very successful, for instance, by working very fast. When it acquired the third largest white goods manufacturer in the USA, White Consolidated, negotiations were concluded within a week. The Zanussi Group, which was bankrupt, reached breakeven point only a year after the takeover. This speed is achieved by using task forces, groups of three or four people who visit the new partner and review it for potential synergies in purchasing, production

1985	Zanker	West Germany
	Beijer Bygg	Sweden
	Duo-Therm	USA
	Staub/BM	France
	Righton	Great Britain
1986	White	USA
	Gotthard	Sweden
	Poulan/WE	USA
1987	Tricity/Scott Benham	Great Britain
	D & M	USA
	AKTA	Sweden
1988	Corberó/Domar	Spain
	Unidad Hermética	Spain
	Briax/Kolb/Cooldr.	UK/W. Germany/Australia
	A&E System	USA
	Alpeninox	Italy
	American Yard Prod.	USA

Figure P.1 *The major acquisitions of Electrolux 1985–88*

and sales. Electrolux also pursues a policy of widespread decentralization and great flexibility within its overall approach. Its unconventional, occasionally even courageous, behaviour also contributes to its success. For example, when Werthén visits his national directors he often asks them 'What would you do if it came to the crunch?' The ideas produced in these brainstorming sessions are not infrequently put into practice.

The success of Electrolux, then, has had nothing to do with perfecting its existing activities. Instead the company engaged in a systematic, and therefore successful, search for opportunities to expand in completely new ways. It has not made isolated takeovers but has turned the process of repeated takeover and restructuring into the backbone of its strategy. In the last twenty years Electrolux has acquired and restructured no fewer than 400 firms, of various sizes. Repeating the process so often has given Electrolux a unique skill which is one of the basic requirements for effective expansion.

Glaxo: How to overtake the world leaders in pharmaceuticals

In 1979 Glaxo was just a medium-sized British chemicals concern with a turnover of £539m. in pharmaceuticals, food products, specialized chemicals, and agricultural and horticultural products. In 1988 its turnover, achieved almost exclusively with pharmaceuticals, was £2,059m. This dynamic expansion in the space of a few years made Glaxo the second largest pharmaceutical manufacturer in the world. Only the American company Merck had not been ousted from its leading position. All the other well-known manufacturers – Hoechst (No. 2 in 1981), Ciba-Geigy (No. 2 in 1987), American Hospital (No. 2 in 1984), etc. – were overtaken with ease. Figure P.2 shows Glaxo's meteoric rise.

	1985	1986	1987	1988
1	Merck	Merck	Merck	Merck
2	American H.	Ciba-Geigy	Ciba-Geigy	**Glaxo**
3	Ciba-Geigy	American H.	**Glaxo**	Ciba-Geigy
4	SKB	SKB	American H.	American H.
5	Pfizer	Hoechst	Hoechst	Hoechst
6	J&J	Pfizer	SKB	SKB
7	Hoechst	**Glaxo**	Pfizer	Pfizer
8	Eli Lilly	J&J	J&J	Sandoz
9	Bristol-Myers	Eli Lilly	Sandoz	Eli Lilly
10	Roche	Sandoz	Eli Lilly	Bayer

Figure P.2 *The 'top ten' pharmaceutical producers*

In those ten years the after tax profit climbed from £47m. to £571m. Dividend payments increased from £13m. in 1979 to £185m. in 1988. Tax revenue for the state rose from £25m. in 1979 to £261m. in 1988.

With Glaxo we see again that expansion has been enormously beneficial both for the workforce (attractive jobs, opportunities for personal development) and for the shareholders and the state. Above all, the customers have profited from the firm's performance. For example, Glaxo developed and now supplies a drug called Zantac which is used for infections of the stomach lining and has helped to reduce the number of operations on stomach ulcers.

What is the 'secret' of this dynamic growth?

One milestone was the appointment of Sir Paul Girolami to head the management team in 1980. He decided on a number of dramatic changes of direction, including concentration on pharmaceuticals. In the 1980s all non-pharmaceutical activities were relinquished.

Girolami's main contribution, however, was his innovative approach to pharmaceutical sales. Before 1980 no pharmaceutical manufacturer would have dreamt of handing over the sale of a product it had developed to another pharmaceutical manufacturer. But Girolami was determined that the drug Ranitidin (which was first registered in the 1970s and is principally supplied under the brand name Zantac) should be introduced as fast as possible into the maximum number of markets in order to make the most of the relatively short period of patent protection. Building up Glaxo's own sales force would have taken far too long.

Girolami recognized the potential of cooperating with other pharmaceutical organizations. In a very short time cooperation deals had been struck with a number of pharmaceutical firms. In the USA, for instance, Zantac was sold by three separate organizations, which enabled Glaxo to treble its turnover in the USA, from £66m. in 1983 to £193m. in 1984, and to attain a turnover of £831m. within the next five years. That single decision to cooperate with other pharmaceutical firms – in Glaxo they call it 'co-marketing' – led not only to unimaginable expansion but also to some uniquely strong returns (pre-tax profit 40 per cent of turnover in 1988!)

Girolami discovered further latent potential in the organizational procedure which Glaxo used for the registration of new drugs. Until the end of the 1970s Glaxo, in common with practically all the other pharmaceutical firms, registered new drugs in its home market to begin with, and only then ventured to register them abroad. Girolami decided that Ranitidin should be registered simultaneously in all the important markets of the world. This change from the customary sequential registration (one country after another) to parallel registration constituted a significant innovation.

Of course Glaxo's success can also be attributed to the efficacy of its drugs, particularly the newly developed Ranitidin. Zantac, to use the brand name, does have certain advantages over its rival, Tagamet, produced by Smith-Kline Beckmann. For instance, it only has to be taken twice a day, in contrast to Tagamet's four times. This competitive advantage alone, however, cannot possibly account for the scale of Glaxo's success.

The moral of the story

If we look at these two examples a series of parallels become apparent.

Both firms have shot up the league table. Both started out relatively static, playing a subordinate role in their respective industries. Within a relatively short time, however, they had metamorphosed. Electrolux became the world's biggest supplier of white goods. Glaxo established itself in second place among the pharmaceutical giants.

What is most important is not the growth in their turnover, but the fact that many groups with an interest in the companies – the so-called stakeholders – have gained a great deal. This breakthrough into the big league has benefited customers (high quality products), employees (new job opportunities), management (openings for self-development), and even suppliers (expanding and reliable business), the state (higher taxes and other contributions), and not least the shareholders (higher dividends and share prices). These two examples show how dynamic companies substantially increase value for their stakeholders.

What they also have in common is the way they achieved their breakthrough.

One could simply say, in the conventional way, that both companies skilfully exploited the relevant market potential – Electrolux for white goods and Glaxo for pharmaceuticals. But closer analysis soon reveals that market potential was not the key. Hans Werthén recognized the potential that lay in taking over and restructuring white goods companies. Sir Paul Girolami was the first to tap the enormous potential of cooperation, with his co-marketing strategy. He also took an innovative approach to the whole process of product registration. Werthén subsequently multiplied the process of acquisition and restructuring and used it over 400 times. Girolami multiplied the processes of cooperation in co-marketing.

Let us compare the way these companies' rivals acted.

In the white goods sector, many German and Italian manufacturers concentrated on trying to penetrate the domestic market more intensively. Electrolux chose a completely different strategy. It remained in the same field of business but branched out into a new kind of activity: not the classic market penetration (trying to sell more of the current products to the existing markets), but the takeover and restructuring of its former rivals. Its net profit shot up because it dramatically increased the yield of the companies it took over and reorganized. This new business concept is the main difference between Electrolux and most of its German and Italian rivals, but to be able to put it into practice Electrolux needed much more. It needed to have a fresh, enterprising business approach, to search carefully for new, unconventional ways of adding value of all kinds, and to make dynamic use of the opportunities it found.

In the same way Glaxo's success springs above all from its new, cooperative approach to the market, co-marketing, and from an organizational revolution, parallel registration. Neither of these would have been possible without the new, enterprising philosophy which encouraged such flexible, unconventional and creative steps. The traditional pharmaceutical manufacturers, by contrast, stuck to conventional management styles, which led only to stagnation and missed opportunities.

To sum up: dynamic companies diverge from their conventional rivals by creating fresh paths to new opportunities. This is the heart of corporate dynamism.

Note

1 Hirn, 1988, p.67.

Part I

The principles
of dynamic development

Chapter 1

Corporate dynamism: management for the future

The challenge of change

In recent years the business world has become more and more unsettled.

- Economic developments such as the coming single European market, the Third World debt crisis, exchange rate fluctuations and so on are forcing companies to adapt quickly.
- Political developments and new legislation can change the ground rules. Even developments in other countries, such as the liberalization of Eastern Europe (or reactions against it), can affect our own economic situation.
- For many companies the phenomenal advances in technology in the last few years present a particular challenge.
- Environmental issues are rapidly gaining importance.
- Social trends such as population growth (stagnating in most industrial nations but still exploding in the Third World) and hedonism will become more and more important.

These developments can mean rapid, dramatic changes in supply and demand, as well as in the financial and labour markets. One result of the turbulent climate has been the growing number of takeovers. Another is the surprising speed with which companies which were once at the top of the tree can lose their commanding positions or disappear altogether. Thus, for example, 53 of the top 100 firms in the Fortune 500 list for 1966 were not among the top 100 in 1986. Of the 47 firms remaining 23 held lower positions.

Change offers opportunities as well as dangers. The successful company will not only fend off the dangers, but will also seize the opportunities and make the most of them. The only rule is this: the more changeable the environment and the market, the faster the company must adapt. Hence the growing importance of dynamism: only dynamic companies can exploit the opportunities in such a way that all their stakeholders are much better off.

Unfortunately, many businesses overlook this simple concept. For various reasons, instead of looking to the long term and exploiting opportunities they go onto the defensive. Managements try to protect themselves against the uncertainties of the outside world by using bureaucratic control. The gap widens between what the world requires and what the company delivers: the company cannot fail to miss the boat, and sink without trace. So in a turbulent climate corporate dynamism is essential to success.

Benefits for all stakeholders: the measure of dynamism

We have seen that dynamic companies make flexible use of the opportunities presented by a climate of change, but that is not their only distinguishing characteristic. The examples of Electrolux and Glaxo show that above all dynamic firms generate wealth: their dynamism means that value is greatly increased. This gives us our basic definition.

By a dynamic company we mean an economic entity which considerably increases the benefits for its stakeholders within a relatively short time.

This definition needs to be amplified a little:

The crucial point is that all the stakeholders should benefit, that is, all those people and organizations who have an interest in the wellbeing of the company (from employees through shareholders to customers and suppliers).[1] As a rule the dynamic company generates value not for just one group of stakeholders (say, shareholders), but equally for everyone.

Time is also an important factor. With dynamism the increase in value can be achieved quite quickly, usually within a few years.

The concept of a 'dynamic company' is closely linked with the expression 'corporate dynamism'. This implies a specific, dynamically oriented corporate structure and a corresponding management style.

Corporate dynamism could therefore be defined as a way of developing a company so that all its stakeholders are several times better off in a relatively short time.

With the aid of these somewhat pragmatic definitions and plenty of empirical observation we shall investigate the nature of corporate dynamism. The object of this book is to offer entrepreneurs, captains of industry and entrepreneurial managers some guidelines on dynamic management. We shall look at the principles which dynamic companies apply, and consider how to manage a dynamic company.

Is dynamic growth really desirable?

This is a time when much consideration is being given, quite rightly, to the limits of what mankind can and should do. Quantitative growth is viewed with increasing suspicion. Yet here I am, putting forward expansionist principles. Is it appropriate to take such an attitude now?

I will approach this topic from four angles:

- The economic situation
- The type of growth
- Competition
- The workforce.

In many countries the *economic situation* is still coloured by uncertainty, stagnation, high unemployment and, often, poverty. Rampant bureaucracy gets in the way of long-term development. In all these countries the wellbeing of the inhabitants depends on economic development. Businesses are needed – the more the better – which can relatively quickly increase the benefits for their stakeholders several times over. These benefits would take the form of job creation, more orders for suppliers, a higher tax revenue and, not least, higher yields for shareholders and owners. So it is dynamic companies which can best help solve the economic problems which hang over many countries. Dynamic growth generally entails dispensing with bureaucracy, and that too can make both private and public sector organizations stronger.

As for the *type of growth*, the current wave of criticism mainly concerns quantitative growth. Dynamic expansion, however, is not primarily quantitative; on the contrary, nowadays added value is very often qualitative: products are improved and valuable new services are offered. Extra value stems increasingly from software rather than hardware performance. In many cases business expansion actually leads to less raw material being used. This is clearly seen where dynamic development consists in taking over and restructuring 'undermanaged companies'.[2] In the same way an example from the motor industry illustrates the optimized use of materials. In 1975 a Cadillac DeVille Sedan weighed 2,355 kg. After the oil price crisis the company changed direction and this weight was reduced by 37 per cent, to 1,495 kg. in 1987. Expansion should not, therefore, be equated with forced quantitative growth. On the contrary, skilful expansion focuses on quality.

In a *competitive world* dynamism is of course essential to survival. Dynamic companies can adapt more easily to follow new trends, which inevitably leads to competitive advantages and increased market share.

Finally, corporate dynamism is important for the *workforce*. The object of any company's activities is to generate wealth. Dynamic companies generate above-average wealth and benefit all their stakeholders, so there is real purpose to their activities. Employees identify strongly with such a company and are highly motivated. Besides, corporate dynamism is geared to the long term: employees can see that the company is prospering and opening up new opportunities for their personal development. This is another motivating influence. For instance, when the Bank in Liechtenstein created over 300 per cent new jobs between 1980 and 1988, many employees were able to move up into higher, more responsible management positions. It is not just the promotion prospects which are motivating: success leads to pride in the company and a strong sense of identity, important ingredients of job satisfaction.

On balance, then, dynamic development means resources are used more efficiently and creatively. Wastage is fundamentally contrary to the spirit of dynamic growth, so healthy business dynamics and a healthier environment go hand in hand. Corporate dynamism is essentially positive, and it would be shortsighted to reject it because of a blanket hostility to growth.

How to make a company dynamic

As a rule a company can take two possible approaches to dynamism: on the one hand it can take measures in the field of organization and man-management and on the other it can attempt to enhance the value it generates.

Publications on the subject of corporate dynamism have been surprisingly scarce to date, and what there is deals mostly with the area of organization and man-management.[3] Dynamism is seen to spring from a certain management style, usually practised by a manager with a naturally 'dynamic' personality. Some rules are recommended, such as:

- Set ambitious goals which can be achieved in a short time.
- Initiate a bias for action.
- Make sure your corporate culture encourages high performance and speed.

- Motivate your staff in every way possible, eg by offering high productivity bonuses.
- Make your organizational structure a flat one and delegate widely.

In other words it is up to the manager to make the organization dynamic.

There is, however, an alternative approach based on the philosophy that dynamics can be generated by exploiting potential, and that the overriding aim should be to increase value for all stakeholders. Roughly speaking, if the company is producing worthwhile goods or services, dynamic growth happens almost by itself. In extreme cases there is no need at all for the influence of a 'dynamic' manager, since the company is simply drawn into expansion by the demand for its products. For instance, if a company produces an innovative product which is much better than the competition, this product will be practically torn out of its hands. The management won't need to apply any pressure: the customers will make the workforce dynamic.

It is extremely difficult to energize a company simply by organization and motivation, and I feel that the dynamic company should ideally combine both approaches. Corporate dynamism should be founded on activities which generate wealth by exploiting promising value potential, a concept I shall explain more fully later. At the same time, organizational and motivational steps should be taken to release the latent expansionist forces in the company. Figure 1.1 shows the three approaches to dynamic development.

The essence of dynamism

Any analysis of business dynamics should start on the conceptual level, for it is here that the right conditions are created for dynamism to develop on other levels. So let us look at the generation of wealth, particularly three features prominent in corporate dynamism which have so far received little attention in management theory.

1   Dynamic companies need to *concentrate on promising value potential*. Electrolux found value potential in medium-sized white goods companies which could be taken over and restructured.
2   The activities which tap the value potential must be *multiplied*. Using our previous example again: it was not enough for Electrolux to take over one single white goods company. It achieved the professionalism which led to much higher profits only by carrying out a number of takeovers.
3   These two elements are accompanied by a third: corporate dynamism

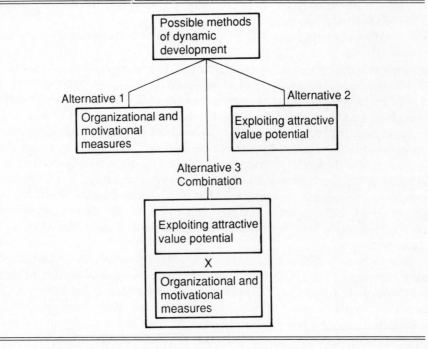

Figure 1.1 *Three approaches to dynamic development*

is always induced by someone with an enterprising personality, a *growth promoter*.

These three elements form the cornerstones of dynamic development. The principle of dynamism is this: value potential is recognized by a growth promoter under whose guidance it is multiply exploited. The following examples show just how important those cornerstones are.

Value potential

In 1964 two British transport firms, Oswald Tillotson and Commercial Motors, were taken over by the Wiles Group for £900,000. As a result the Chairman of Tillotson, James Edward Hanson (now Lord Hanson), and his chief executive, Gordon (now Sir Gordon) White, moved onto the board of the parent company. At that time the Wiles Group was making an after tax profit of about £75,000. However, Hanson realized that in the long term no interesting opportunities were likely to arise in that field of business, and he would have to reckon with a decline in profits.

Hanson had become convinced back in the 1950s that British companies were far from efficiently managed. Socialist measures brought in under the Labour government had crippled management, and in many firms managers were lamenting the 'good old days'. Passivity and resignation were rife. The gulf between management and workers was visibly widening. Lord Hanson saw in all this a wonderful opportunity, and together with Sir Gordon White changed the Wiles Group into a holding company. From the mid-1960s this holding company repeatedly bought up and reorganized 'undermanaged companies', in some cases selling them off again later.

In 1969 the name of the company was changed to the Hanson Trust, and since 1988 the group has traded under the name Hanson plc. It has become one of the most dynamic and successful companies there is. In the financial year to 1988 Hanson plc achieved a turnover of £7,400m. and record profits of £880m. Lord Hanson wrote proudly in the Annual Report for 1988: '25 years of sustained growth'.

This is a practical example of the nature of dynamic development. Lord Hanson could have stuck with his transport company and battled on, but he recognized that its growth and profit potential was limited and looked for new opportunities instead. He found them in 'undermanaged companies', which could be acquired for bargain prices. Great rewards beckoned anyone who would take on the task of reorganizing them: the value of his company could be enormously increased.

Lord Hanson's success springs from the fact that he recognized the potential, in Britain in the 1960s, of 'undermanaged companies'. This potential enabled him to generate great value – in other words, it was tremendous value potential.

The logical consequence of all this is that not only Lord Hanson and his shareholders, who now number over 200,000, profited from the value potential. Hanson plc has become one of the most important taxpayers in Britain and hence created considerable wealth for the nation. More than 100,000 employees have interesting jobs. Many managers have found opportunities for advancement in this dynamic organization. And suppliers have a stable business partner in Hanson plc.

The dynamic company must be able to find and develop attractive value potential. Without it the company will be wasting its effort, swimming against the tide. Value potential can be found in a wide variety of areas. The best known is surely market potential, meaning untapped demand, which is still the focal point of most management. But other kinds of value potential can offer dynamic companies the opportunity for enormous profit. For example, the extreme liquidity of capital markets all over the world in the early 1980s opened up enormous potential for innovative forms of financing, which was systematically exploited through leveraged buyouts, venture capital financing and so on. Firms which are quick to identify and exploit innovative and attractive value potential can achieve great momentum.

Multiplication

The second component of corporate dynamism is multiplication. Repeating the activity which exploits value potential is the only way to keep the dynamic forces going; it has a cumulative effect far greater than that of carrying out a number of different kinds of activity.

Hanson plc multiplied the processes of acquiring and restructuring companies. We have also seen multiplication in the examples in the Prologue: Electrolux worked in the same way as Hanson, only multiplying the acquisition and restructuring of white goods companies. Glaxo simultaneously multiplied several different activities which exploited the market potential for innovative drugs:

- Firstly the processes of cooperation, in the form of co-marketing, were multiplied as part of a general strategy of globalization. Glaxo entered into joint ventures with several pharmaceutical companies, eg Hoffmann–La Roche.
- Secondly Glaxo multiplied the process of registering drugs more quickly.
- Thirdly it multiplied production facilities and production processes, building factories in thirty different countries.

The best dynamics are generated only by repeatedly exploiting value potential in this way. If Glaxo had simply sold Zantac in its traditional market (which in the late 1970s was predominantly Great Britain and the Commonwealth), its stakeholders would not have benefited nearly so much. Success would have been short-lived, and there would have been great danger of the dynamic development slowing down. So multiplication is an essential part of dynamic development.

The principle is this: management activities to generate dynamic growth are only really effective within a framework of multiplication. For multiplication to be efficient organizational structures need to be fairly autonomous and flexible.

The growth promoter

In 1955, Ray Kroc opened his first restaurant in Illinois. He soon recognized the huge potential that existed in the fast food business and started to exploit the potential systematically. Approximately 30 years later, 'his company', McDonald's, reached $5 billion in revenues. Several years after his death in 1984, Ray Kroc's philosophy is still highly respected at McDonald's.

Ray Kroc was very practically oriented and dropped out of high school after two years. His talents lay in sales and marketing, and he was an excellent, innovative entrepreneur.

He saw the success potential of combining the principles of franchising with food service standardization and convenience. John Love, the author of a history of McDonald's, explains, 'The essence of Kroc's unique but amazingly simple franchising philosophy was that a franchising company should not live off the sweat of its franchisees, but should succeed by helping its franchises succeed.'[4] The result of his superior ability to select and motivate managers, franchisees and suppliers was a family consisting of 2,500 independent companies with common goals and interests.[5]

Another important success factor was the company's devotion to *quality, service, cleanliness and value*. Mike Quinlan, now Chief Executive Officer, puts it this way: 'If there's one reason for our success, it's that Ray Kroc instilled in the company basic principles. Standards of excellence. Don't compromise. Use the best ingredients. The best equipment.'[6]

Ray Kroc was neither the founder of McDonald's nor the creator of fast food restaurants. However, his creativity in the franchise business was the cornerstone of McDonald's success. Through the multiplication of this value potential, Kroc achieved extremely dynamic growth: the franchise concept was multiplied over 10,000 times. McDonald's has recently added outlets in Moscow and Belgrade and in other Eastern bloc countries to its global operations. The dynamic expansion resulted in over $14 billion in revenues for all restaurants in 1987. McDonald's is now the largest food service corporation in the world and also the largest commercial real estate owner in America.[7]

Here is an outstanding example of an entrepreneurial growth promoter: someone with a vision of a new kind of business and the energy to turn that vision into reality.[8]

Obviously optimal dynamic development depends on the presence of one or more growth promoters. These are the classic entrepreneurs, determined to achieve something, to take on the risks involved and to shape their own future.

The basic structure of dynamic development

We can now see the basic structure of dynamic development, with its three cornerstones:

1   The dynamic company increases value, producing goods or services which are in great demand, so that in the ideal situation the product sells itself, the staff are highly motivated and the company simply has

to expand. To start this process it exploits attractive value potential.

2   Exploiting value potential on a one-off basis can help the company along for a short time, but if there is to be sustained dynamic growth the relevant activities have to be multiplied. This means that the value potential chosen should be of a kind which allows repeated exploitation. Multiplication has a number of advantages with a dynamic effect, for example, economies of scale, which increase efficiency and boost net profits.

3   An entrepreneurial individual, a growth promoter, initiates the dynamic process and ensures continued dynamic growth.

The principles of dynamic growth are shown in Figure 1.2. Correctly applied they can create considerable leverage. Attractive value potential can generate its own momentum, as the company provides output of real value which is easy to sell. This in turn stimulates the company to produce more.

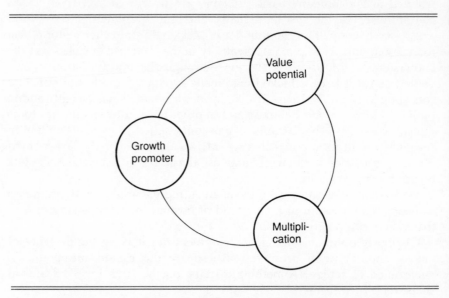

Figure 1.2 *The three cornerstones of corporate dynamism*

Multiplication has a similar effect. Repetition of the company's activities leads to a wide range of improvements in the output. Greater expertise and familiarity mean higher quality, lower costs, and a faster process. Seeing these improvements stimulates the company to search for other opportunities to multiply activities.

Thus the combination of attractive value potential and multiplication gives the company a powerful lever to push it into new dimensions.

Guidelines for management

Benefits for all stakeholders

The dynamic manager sees the purpose of his company as being to generate and increase value for all its stakeholders, ie customers, employees, investors, suppliers and the community at large.

The principles of dynamic development

Entrepreneurial managers act as growth promoters, initiating and multiplying business activities which exploit attractive value potential.

Leverage

Growth promoters trigger off the forces of dynamic growth in two ways:

1   They make the most of the natural stimulative effect of attractive value potential.
2   They exploit the advantages (such as learning curves) of multiplication in the knowledge that these too have a stimulative effect.

The principles of dynamic management are a combination of these elements, whose cumulative effect is a powerful lever to expansion.

Notes

1   Ulrich writes in this context of institutions '...which make or could make some kind of claim on the company' [translated by the present translator]. (1987, p. 66)
2   Cf. Hanson's strategy in the investment report of CIBC Securities Europe Limited, 'A Share for Uncertain Times', January 1988, pp. 12ff.
3   Cf. eg Peters and Waterman (1982), especially 'A Bias for Action'; Mills (1985); Bright (1985); Tichy and Devanna (1986).
4   See Moser, 1988, p. 115.
5   See Love, 1986.
6   See Moser, 1988.
7   Ibid.
8   Cf. also the contribution of Pleitner on the role of the growth promoter in new venture companies: Pleitner (1986, pp. 34-43).

Chapter 2

Value potential: fertile soil for dynamic growth

What is value potential?

Value potential is one of the three cornerstones of dynamic growth: dynamic companies exploit value potential. In the first chapter we saw some examples:

- Glaxo focused on the value potential that lay in cooperating with other pharmaceutical firms.
- Like Electrolux, Hanson exploited the value potential of 'undermanaged companies' which emerged in Britain in the 1960s and 1970s.
- McDonald's tapped the market potential of fast food service.

What do these different kinds of value potential have in common?

Firstly, value potential requires a certain favourable combination of circumstances as evidenced by, for example, a number of 'undermanaged companies' or a number of capital investors. This combination may be found within the company, or it could be in the market or elsewhere in the company's environment. It may not even be an obvious combination as yet.

Secondly, it is something which a company can develop through its business activities to its own advantage and that of all its stakeholders.

Value potential can therefore be defined as a favourable combination of circumstances in the environment or market or within the company that is either still latent or already recognizable. This potential is then exploited through company activities for the benefit of all stakeholders. However, obvious potential of this kind is usually of little interest because it is bound to be noticed and harnessed by other companies as well. For example, there is doubtless great potential in the market for personal computers, but in practice this is only open to PC firms which are already established. Less conspicuous, latent potential benefit is much more interesting. Henry Ford recognized the latent demand for low-priced motor cars at the beginning of this century, and immediately developed a product – the famous Model T – with which to tap the market potential. It is worth noting in this context that, in a large market, value potential may often arise in the form of market niches.

For corporate dynamism, value potential is only of interest if it will allow many transactions. We have seen that in the 1970s there were a number of white goods firms in need of restructuring, and their value potential was very attractive for Electrolux. Over the years this potential has been extensively exploited and hence lost its attraction, so that Electrolux will have to scout round for new, attractive value potential. The level of attraction must always be judged from the point of view of your own company. Even a large potential market can be unattractive if too many competitors are involved, reducing the possible profits.

It should be clear by now why I have introduced this new term, 'value potential'. Familiar terms such as market potential or profit potential do not go far enough. I should like to clarify this and make the necessary distinctions between the various terms.

Classic, market-oriented management theory focuses on the relationship between the company and the market. The company is perceived as a productive social system which provides goods or services for a third party – the market.[1] This is also true in strategic theory, where the competitive dimension is taken into account. One of the main objectives of 'competitive strategy'[2] is to achieve superiority over the competition by creating the right emphasis.

This model inevitably places great weight on market potential. To put it simply, the company must concentrate on markets with considerable potential and offer these markets products which are better than those of the competition. The basic model is illustrated in Figure 2.1.

Market potential plays an important role in dynamic development, too. But dynamic growth can also be generated by tapping other types of potential, so every kind of potential open to the company should be taken into consideration. I have already mentioned the potential of companies in need of reorganization; other interesting sources of potential can be the capital market and the labour market. Value potential can even be found within the company itself, in the shape of untapped expertise, unexploited synergies or assets which could be better deployed.

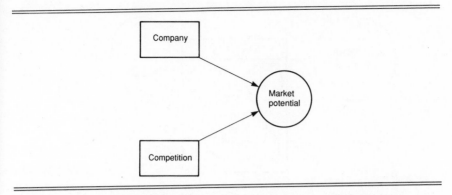

Figure 2.1 *The basic model of competitive strategy: a company competes with one or more rivals to tap into market potential*

'Value potential' should therefore be thought of as a generic term, including market potential as just one type of potential among many others. Figure 2.2 shows the broader base of this approach compared with the classic management approach of Figure 2.1. The principles of corporate dynamism differ from classic competitive strategy and should be seen as a complete corporate concept.[3]

Nor would the more common expression 'profit potential' be appropriate to the concept. In the end, of course, any company trying to be dynamic is also trying to increase its own profits, but instead of working entirely to the advantage of its shareholders it must increase benefits for all its stakeholders at once. It must achieve a balance which will avoid conflicts and give higher value to all its stakeholders, including its investors. This is why we must talk, not of conventional profit potential, but, in a wider sense, of value potential.

I have written previously about 'strategic excellence positions', where companies consciously develop selected skills which give them superiority over the competition and hence above-average results over the long term.[4] Here the focus is on the company's skills, in contrast with value potential, where the focus falls on a grouping in the environment or the market, or possibly within the company. It is often necessary to build up strategic excellence positions in order to exploit long-running value potential.

In short, the existing terms all express ideas which are quite distinct from 'value potential' as I perceive it.

Only limited growth can be achieved by 'dynamic behaviour' and hectic activity. It is crucial to dynamic growth that the company's activities should be directed towards areas where yields are high. In other words, dynamic growth can only be sustained when the company's activities generate high value.

For example: *Club Méditerranée* primarily exploits the market potential

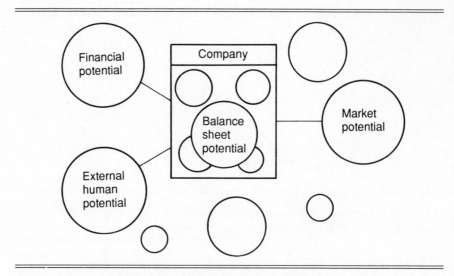

Figure 2.2 *The basic model of the dynamic approach*
The company concentrates on tapping value potential which is attractive (and will accordingly not just be market potential). In this illustration the company is exploiting four types of value potential:
- *External value potential: financial potential, market potential, external human potential*
- *Internal value potential: balance sheet potential*

It is ignoring any other value potential. The size of the circles indicates how attractive each is.

for holidays. Its club idea (inclusive price, relaxed atmosphere, sports facilities, entertainment, good food and so on) is the perfect product. Attractive value potential, combined with excellent customer service, means that Club Med's stakeholders all do well out of it. Its customers enjoy their holidays. Shareholders saw share prices rise from 110 FFr. in 1983 to 700 FFr. in 1987. Turnover increased in the same period by 37%. The Club has also helped the developing countries in which it has built its holiday villages, opening up, for example, many educational opportunities for the indigenous population.

Club Med has also discovered value potential in the labour market when it comes to recruiting GOs (*gentils organisateurs*, the company's representatives in the club villages). The prospect of working in the holiday atmosphere of the villages is so appealing that the Club receives 100,000 applications every year, despite the relatively low pay. At present only 2,000 applications can be considered. The advantages of this value potential include lower recruitment and personnel costs and high-quality GOs.

This potential in the labour market – external human potential – has a stimulative effect: it is easier to set up a new village in the knowledge that manpower will not be a problem. Customer demand, too, remains strong enough to encourage expansion; the club concept is still a popular innovation and Club Med can rely on high booking levels.

This is an example of attractive value potential building up momentum, so that the company's development is virtually self-propelled: a very high-value product stimulates disproportionate demand, which encourages dynamic growth. In the early days of Club Med, Gilbert Trigano would arrive at Head Office early in the morning to find throngs of customers queuing to be sure of a place in their favourite village. Many had been there since four o'clock. Experiences such as this, and the demand for jobs as GOs, made him expand, planning and opening new villages. A company which taps attractive value potential is naturally energized. It simply cannot become rigid and bureaucratic.

Value potential, then, is the true breeding-ground of dynamic development. The dynamic company must identify and exploit value potential, at the same time giving up any potential which is losing its attraction.

Many static companies work in the opposite direction. When the value they generate declines as part of the natural cycle, they become ever more defensive. Within the company they try to control the situation by regulations, intensive monitoring and other bureaucratic measures, while externally they lobby the state or other 'sponsors' to protect them. Trade restrictions are demanded, and subsidies, both open and secret, are used to maintain the status quo. Unfortunately the end result is always disadvantageous as we have seen in the coal and steel industry, agriculture, weapon manufacture, and, in West Germany, in telecommunications. Defensive measures of this kind only work for a short time, breaking down altogether when the product becomes so unprofitable that the industry's backers are no longer prepared to support it.

Where does value potential come from?

At the beginning of this chapter I stressed that the dynamic company concentrates on *attractive* value potential, which provides scope for a number of profitable business transactions. The scope is always reduced where other companies are competing to exploit the potential in question.

For this reason value potential is always at its most interesting when it is only just taking shape or has not yet been discovered. The first company to exploit potential has the greatest chance of expansion and high rewards, so it is important to establish how new value potential arises.

My research indicates that as a rule new value potential is the result of changes – in the environment, in the markets or in the company itself. A shift of the parameters causes an imbalance, which creates an arena for possible innovative business activities. Taking the case of Electrolux: many smaller white goods companies were underutilizing their production capacity, which meant that their production costs were too high for the prices they could achieve in a saturated market. Electrolux was able to even out the imbalance by merging production facilities and by other reorganizational measures, thereby guaranteeing better use of capacity.

So new value potential nearly always springs from new developments in the business environment, in the market or in the company itself. The entrepreneur must gain control of changes and shifting coordinates and their repercussions for the company.

Different, often unique, developments occur all the time, and it is difficult to predict which value potential holds most promise for the future. Dynamic companies have a creative approach: they keep constant watch for new value potential in all areas, not just the sales markets. In this way they uncover opportunities which remain hidden from static companies.

Unfortunately, many companies have become set in their ways after decades in the same line of business. Managers are fixated on market potential, even when it is disappearing. Few are flexible enough to consider other kinds of potential.

The phases of value potential

Changes in the business climate, the market and the company mean that value potential evolves over time, rather than remaining static. Often potential goes through a cycle, of emergence, growth, maturity and decline.

Of course value potential does not often follow a strict pattern; it can develop in very different ways. In many cases the growth phase never arrives, though there are situations in which it can last a surprisingly long time. Bayer's drug aspirin has been available in powder form since 1900, yet even today new therapeutic effects are being discovered, further extending the indications for its use.[5] In other product groups, for instance in many foodstuffs, there can be a long, stagnant, mature phase as the potential levels out. There can also be startling oscillations in demand.

The cyclic model, then, is a very broad generalization, but a useful one. The dynamic company will face different problems and challenges according to the development phase its value potential has reached. Let us examine the four typical phases of development in turn.

Relatively little business volume can be generated from value potential in its *emergent phase*, for two reasons. Firstly, the changes which give rise to the value potential are at an early stage themselves. For example, in the late 1970s the potential for personal computers was slight, since microprocessors at that time were not very powerful. Similarly, the junk bond was not seen as a serious financial instrument at the beginning of the 1980s, so leveraged buyouts could not readily be introduced at that stage. Secondly, the company itself has had little opportunity to learn how to make most effective use of the value potential.

It is in the *growth phase* that both outside influences and the company's own experience really come into their own. In the PC market technological progress led to the development of increasingly powerful microprocessors. By the introduction of Intel 8086 in 1979, which meant that personal computers could at last be widely used, much had been learnt about how to harness the potential. IBM, for instance, became very good at marketing, developing the Charlie Chaplin campaign which was so successful.

In the growth phase, too, business transactions tend to increase in size. The first leveraged buyouts cost less than \$100m., whereas the RJR–Nabisco takeover at the end of 1988 ran to no less than \$24,500m.

In the *maturity phase* a whole series of factors can lead to a slowdown, as changes in the business environment cause the value potential to dry up. This is often seen with technological potential: the introduction of electronic clocks meant that the market for mechanical clocks was glutted and later shrank dramatically. Maturity can also arise as a profitable product is more widely distributed, leading to saturation in the markets for washing machines, dishwashers and so on, for example. Increasing competition can mean reduced potential. Of course internal potential, say, company takeovers, is just as prone to maturity as market potential. There is an obvious limit to the number of assets that can be redeployed.

These trends continue into the *decline phase*. A shrinking market means declining market potential, while internal potential declines as possibilities for further asset disposals or reorganizations are exhausted.

Value potential typically develops in a cyclic curve, as shown in Figure 2.3. The profits earned from value potential follow a similar curve. In the emergent phase there is considerable expenditure, leading to negative results. Breakeven and the first profits are usually reached during the growth phase. As the value potential matures and starts to decline profits may still be high for a while, before dropping off and possibly even turning into losses as potential dwindles and competition grows.

The crucial point here is the close relationship between the development phase of the value potential in question and corporate dynamism. Dynamics are much easier to generate where attractive value potential is concerned, and the most successful dynamic growth is achieved by companies tapping into value potential in the transition between emergence and growth, or even in the middle of the growth phase.

Cyclic models have been used in all kinds of areas before, such as product life cycles, new venture management[6] or organizational models.[7]

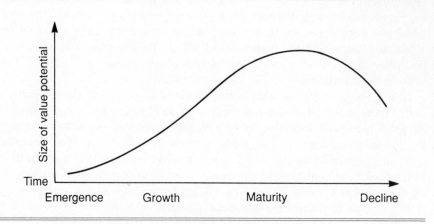

Figure 2.3 *The phases of value potential*

This one is useful because it helps us to see how the attraction of value potential varies, and to relate it to developments in the business world. We can look at the important trends and work out how they are likely to affect value potential which might now or later be of interest to our company.

Many companies already analyse world trends and their consequences, but primarily from the product–market angle. This is a serious mistake, as the ensuing typical example will show. After that I shall go on to analyse the most important current trends and their effects on value potential.

World trends and value potential: The case of Mepa GmbH, Augsburg[8]

In April 1983 I had a phone call from a Mr Fuchs, owner and managing director of Mepa GmbH in Augsburg, one of the leading German manufacturers of metal packaging. Fuchs was very impressed by John Naisbitt's newly published *Megatrends*, which he had just bought while on a trip to the USA. He wanted me to join him and close colleagues in an analysis of the opportunities and threats presented to his company by the trends Naisbitt described. I thought this would be a fascinating exercise and willingly agreed to take part in the one-day workshop.

All the participants were given a copy of Naisbitt's book in advance of the conference and asked to study it carefully and think about the possible effects of the megatrends on their company.

At the start of the day each member of management briefly presented their conclusions. Surprisingly, every single presentation centred on the effects of the megatrends on the manufacture and sales of metal packaging, raising questions such as:

- What does the arrival of new materials mean for us?
- Do we need to include synthetic packaging in our range?
- Should our products be 'greener'?
- How does increased purchasing power affect the market for metal packaging?
- What does the trend 'from representative to participative democracy'[9] signify for our company and our customers?

Hardly anyone had considered anything except the production and sales of metal packaging and the whole day was spent discussing it. In the end they decided to diversify into synthetic packaging, a project which was quickly initialized. However, the competition in this field was already fierce, many other companies having established strong strategic positions in the market. Mepa is still struggling and has yet to make a real breakthrough.

The question is: What would have been the dynamic approach? Naisbitt's megatrends were surely a good starting point, but the analysis should have extended beyond the production and sales of metal packaging to all the value potential relevant to Mepa. Ideas might have been considered such as:

- The trend towards services: Could the data processing systems we have developed be offered to others?
- The trend towards independent enterprise: The company is quite large. Could it be subdivided into autonomous new companies in the charge of the most able managers?
- The trend towards small units (small is beautiful): Should small, decentralized production units be built close to the customers?

Widening the perspective in this way might well have uncovered truly innovative value potential which would have held much more attraction than the market for metal and synthetic packaging.

Of course clever entrepreneurs have always come up with ideas like this. There are copious practical examples, not least in the companies where we did our research. But at the same time thinking in the majority of companies today runs along tramlines defined only by the products they manufacture and the markets they sell to. In times of economic uncertainty and above all in the face of impending recession, unconventional, lateral thinking which considers all possible kinds of value potential is more than ever essential. That is one of the key messages of this book.

World trends and value potential: Ten megatrends and their effect on value potential

In this section I shall outline some of the relevant trends for the future and attempt to assess what value potential will be most important as we move towards the twenty-first century, bearing in mind that any prediction is inevitably uncertain, especially when developments are very rapid.

The aim of this section, therefore, is not so much an accurate forecast of the significant trends, as an illustration of the kind of thinking that lies at the root of corporate dynamism. The trends are drawn from the relevant works of some futurologists.[10]

These are the ten trends I shall examine:

1   Surges of growth alternating with periods of recession.
2   Marked fluctuations in monetary supply and economic values.
3   Continuing internationalization and globalization.
4   Very rapid technological advances.
5   Changes in business processes because of new information and communications systems.
6   Significant demographic changes.
7   New social attitudes.
8   Increasing concern about the environment.
9   A new era in East–West relations.
10   The increasing economic importance of the Pacific Basin.

Trend 1: Surges of growth alternating with periods of recession

The growth trend which began after the Second World War was rudely interrupted by the first oil price shock. Since then there have been considerable variations in the world economy. A brief period of expansion in the second half of the 1970s was followed by renewed recession, which was triggered off by the second oil price shock. Since 1983 there has been a new phase of strong expansion.

A number of factors indicate that this positive underlying trend will continue into the future:

•   Economic integration in Europe and throughout the world is a positive influence.
•   Continuing rapid technological progress supports sustained growth.
•   Innovations, which stimulate growth, can be expected not only in the field of technology, but also in the service sector and other areas.
•   The market economy is established as the most effective economic system. Deregulation and the removal of bureaucratic restrictions encourage growth.

- East–West détente is giving new buoyancy to the world economy.
- The pessimism of the 1970s has been to some extent replaced by a more positive stance.

Of course not all developments are positive. We also have to consider the increasing destruction of the environment, the North–South situation, the Third World debt crisis, weak trade balances, the danger of another oil price shock, terrorism and the unstable political situation in the Middle East and the Third World.

The effect on value potential

The first impact of any developments in the world economy is on market potential, of course. The positive growth phase should mean that many markets will grow in the future. On the other hand a number of consumer markets are tending towards saturation, so that market potential is limited.

In many branches of industry there is considerable overcapacity, leading to constant pressure on prices. Overcapacity in the motor industry, for example, has been estimated at over 25 per cent in the 1990s. Much the same goes for the textile, chemical and machine industries. Even in strongly expanding high-tech sectors such as the manufacture of computers and semiconductors capacity is expanding faster than demand, and prices are being forced down to dangerous levels.[11]

Responsible companies therefore need to be wary of opportunities arising purely from economic growth. They must bear in mind not only the competition, but also any possible relapses in case of recession. The key question for many established companies is this: Will the market potential your company is currently exploiting still be attractive in the future, or are overcapacity and competitive pressure going to mean narrower margins? If the market potential, even in the long term, will only permit a yield on capital which is less than the yield on fixed-interest securities, then it is time to turn to other areas of value potential with greater prospects of profit.

Recessions above all open up takeover and reorganization potential. Companies which have specialized in this have sometimes been able to achieve spectacular success, like our two examples of Hanson and Electrolux, as well as the Frenchman, Bernard Tapie, who was well known as a restructurer in the crisis of the early 1980s.[12]

There can also be interesting potential – depending on the prevailing economic climate – in the field of finance. Many companies can take new opportunities by going public – or indeed by going private.

It is already apparent that economic developments can offer dynamic companies plenty of value potential which is more attractive than the potential markets.

Trend 2: Marked fluctuations in monetary supply and economic values

Since the transition from gold parity to a floating dollar in 1973, currency exchange rates have been subject to large fluctuations. Similar swings occur in inflation rates, interest rates, share prices, costs of raw materials, and many other economic values.

Although considerable efforts are being made to even out these swings – some, such as the European exchange rate mechanism, at international level – there are bound to be continuing fluctuations in the future. This fear is founded on a number of factors:

- Globalization entails close economic integration. This, combined with the advances in communications technology, will help to spread local or regional disequilibrium all over the world.
- The amount of investment capital moving freely about in the international finance markets has reached astronomical proportions: in 1988 it was estimated to be about 30 times greater than the movement of goods. Simply moving these monies about can result in substantial imbalances.
- Interactions between paper trading and physical trading have made the markets extremely complex and therefore far more volatile.[13]
- The current balance between companies will be upset as productivity develops at different rates. Many up-and-coming nations, too, are set to catch up with other countries, now beginning to stagnate, and overtake them; all the faster now that expertise can be passed on quickly via new means of communications.
- The supply of land and other physical resources is necessarily limited. In the densely populated industrial nations, in particular, prices rise out of all proportion when purchasing power leads to surges in demand.
- Political turmoil will lead to sudden bottlenecks in supplies of individual goods. Take, for example, the Gulf War of 1991. The Middle East is still unstable, and an oil crisis more damaging than that of 1973 cannot be ruled out. The global repercussions of the War have yet to be fully assessed. There may turn out to be similar developments in other spheres, affecting other goods.

This brief survey is far from complete. There are many other causes of fluctuations, such as droughts which affect food prices and social trends which affect demand. All these have a considerable impact on value potential.

The effect on value potential

According to classic management theory, companies provide a product for third parties. The relationship between company and customer is paramount. Economic output is measured by *added value*, which is the difference between the cost of materials, services and components bought in and the income from products sold. If a company expects significant fluctuations in the economy, then its results will be determined by factors which have nothing to do with adding value – the transformation of goods in the production and sales process. Here are some examples:

* The annual results of a cigar manufacturer will be decisively influenced by the wholesale price of raw tobacco. If it can be bought at low prices then – all other things being equal – there will be a positive surplus. The most efficient production and marketing methods can do little to allay the disadvantages of unfavourable wholesale prices. So the purchasing and management of goods becomes significant value potential, which – ably handled – can be turned to the benefit of the company and other people.
* Price developments affect fixed and current assets. For example, rising land prices can put the company's activities in a completely different light. In many companies a calculation of total costs would soon reveal that rising prices have made the present site unsuitable for the continued manufacture of the goods currently produced. Frequently firms overlook developments such as this. They are simply pleased that their reserves are growing in value and forget that, because the value of their assets is higher, the effective yield on capital, which may have been dramatic hitherto, is being cut. For many Swiss companies, at least, it has actually fallen below the yield on fixed-interest securities. Discrepancies like this attract raiders, at least for quoted companies. It can be a big problem: on the one hand a policy of continuity requires that the company should go on producing the same goods in the same place, while on the other this means insufficient use of growing economic assets. Dynamic companies could look on these 'fallow' assets as value potential and reassess them constantly to see whether they could be put to better use.

Clearly fluctuations in economic values can open up manifold and often overlooked value potential. Dynamic companies are much more flexible than static ones in their use of this value potential.

Trend 3: Continuing internationalization and globalization

Since international markets permit longer production runs, which mean lower unit costs, there has been a clear movement towards the globalization of markets over the last few years.[14] Several factors have encouraged this trend.

Advances in telecommunications have made dramatic cuts in communications costs. Compare the cost of a three-minute phone call from Switzerland to New York in 1935 – 1,374.20 SFr. at 1988 prices – with the cost of a similar call by Telepac, the public data network in 1988 – 0.75 SFr, or 1,832 times less! Transport has also become much cheaper.

Mass communication has also become international. In the city of Zurich, for example, it is now possible to tune in to more than twenty television channels from various European countries and even from overseas. English is becoming even more widespread as a world language, being now the mother tongue of over 400m. people and the second most widely spoken language, after Mandarin Chinese.[15]

An important development in the international arena is the formation of three great economic blocs, North America, Europe, Southeast Asia. The creation of the Single European Market, with 320m. consumers and $4 bn. purchasing power, shows the way.[16] Experts reckon that the growth of the EC in the 1990s, after the removal of its internal borders, will be 5–7 per cent in real terms.[17] Even if the current wave of euphoria about Europe does seem excessive, there is no doubt that the restructuring of the 'old continent' will be a powerful stimulant.

Working in the opposite direction are a number of no less important protectionist tendencies. Restrictions have been placed on the import of Japanese cars into some European countries, as well as the USA, while the extensive non-tariff barriers to trade with Japan are well known.

On balance I think the general trend will still be towards positive integration as long as economic growth continues. It is very much open to question, however, whether it would survive a severe recession.

The effect on value potential

Some of the opportunities of internationalization and globalization are striking: new markets are opening up, there is new market potential to be tapped. This is good news for companies with greater expertise than their foreign rivals. They can exploit not only the external market potential, but also their internal value potential in the shape of knowhow, patents and other protective rights. To make the most of this knowledge, proficiency in development, production and marketing can be practised more widely, following the fashion of setting up sales organizations or production facilities abroad. It is even possible to export whole systems, ideally as franchises, a concept which is already established internationally. Firms such as Benetton, Body Shop, Cartier, H&M, IKEA and McDonald's have succeeded in becoming international by a consistent policy of setting up whole systems in this way.

The most immediate influence of internationalization and globalization may be on market potential, but once again other, equally interesting, value potential springs to mind. Once again there is financial potential in the international finance markets. There can also be interesting human potential. For example: Swissair cannot find enough information scientists in Switzerland. It has found a really original way round this problem, and is joining with other companies (IBM Malaysia and Malaysian Airline System amongst others) to set up a software firm in Kuala Lumpur. This new company will provide software services both for international air travel and for the private and public sectors in Malaysia. Besides strengthening its image through this involvement with a country on the industrial threshold, Swissair is also able to use Malaysian high school graduates, valuable human potential.

I referred above to certain trends running against this progressive internationalization, above all protectionism. Every protectionist measure is supported by interest groups which stand to benefit from it, for protectionist and other political trade barriers also represent a kind of value potential, which I shall call regulation potential. Influencing the political process and hence legislation can often achieve quite considerable advantages. Some industries, such as agriculture, have only really been able to survive because of regulation potential, and many companies have discovered that it can prove very profitable.

However, regulation potential harbours all the dangers of classic protectionism. Relying exclusively on regulation potential is not a good strategy for a dynamic company. In the long term it simply helps to consolidate impractical and uncompetitive structures. I intend only to touch on regulation potential in passing, preferring to concentrate on potential which generates genuine economic benefits.

Increasing internationalization can, of course, have a detrimental effect on existing value potential. Liberalization always leads to a period of fierce competition, and static companies should beware of becoming uncompetitive and having to be sold off as a last resort. This was the situation which faced Therma, for instance, a Swiss white goods manufacturer which had once been highly regarded. It concentrated exclusively on the domestic market, overlooking the trend towards internationalization which started in the 1960s. Larger European suppliers, with better economies of scale and lower costs, started offering products in Switzerland at prices which Therma simply couldn't match. There was no choice but to sell the company to a particularly pressing rival, none other than the Swedish firm, Electrolux. Internationalization and globalization offer two clear alternatives in many sectors: either make the most of the new value potential or disappear from the picture.

Trend 4: Very rapid technological advances

Rapid technological progress is apparent everywhere today. It is most impressive in microelectronics: the number of electronic connections per silicon chip is doubled about every eighteen months. This development ought to continue at least until the year 2000, ensuring an extraordinary increase in the power of computers. Improved processor performance is matched by the development of new software concepts.[18]

New discoveries and applications in chemistry, biotechnology, new materials and other areas will also lead to substantial improvements in products and production processes.

There is a whole series of major discoveries which – each in its own right – may be of just as much importance as the invention of transistors forty years ago:

- Optical computers, which are as much as a thousand times faster than their current electronic forerunners.[19]
- 'Neural networks', which could considerably heighten artificial intelligence.[20]
- Microengineering, the production of absolutely minute machines which could be used for completely new applications.[21]
- Superconductivity, which might open up new electrotechnical applications.

These are just a few hints of the innovations, as yet undreamt of, which may await us in the twenty-first century. They influence every aspect of human life.

The effect on value potential

Technological development is bound to affect market potential, but here we need to be precise.

Some authors advise that product innovation is most likely to be successful if the product is developed in close consultation with the customer.[22] This is certainly true where existing products are being developed further, with the aim of using the improved or new product to penetrate the existing market more intensively. In such a case it is essential to have an explicit market-orientation, as advocated by Tom Peters,[23] for example. To put it in our terminology, it is a question of using the right technological innovations to tap value potential (in this case market potential).

Yet, interestingly enough, there have been a number of successful entrepreneurs in the past who simply developed entirely new products and opened up markets which did not previously exist. Technological innovators such as Thomas Edison, Konrad Zuse, Steve Jobs and Steven Wozniak were anything but market-oriented. They used their specialist knowledge to exploit technology potential and then tried to market the products they had developed. They were very successful, not because of a strategy based on the needs of the customers, but because of the quality of their technological innovation.

The distinction between the customary market-oriented exploitation of market potential which happens to involve new technology on the one hand, and the exploitation of technology potential on the other, seems to me to be an important one. Management research to date indicates that the first way promises more success and is less risky, but there are concrete examples of the second course being more appropriate and successful.

Technological development can also allow the exploitation of internal potential by rationalization or cost-cutting, for example when new machinery increases efficiency.

Trend 5: Changes in business processes due to new information and communications systems

Developments in information and communications systems are, of course, closely connected with the technological progress discussed in the previous section, but their value potential is such that it warrants a section of its own.

Information and communications systems are showing the following tendencies:

- The power of information systems is constantly increasing, with three advantages:
  1 Business processes can be more efficient. Skilful use of information can lead to competitive advantages in costs.
  2 Effective use of information provides a sound basis for decision making, raising the quality of decisions. For example, computer models can be used to work out the highest yield on stocks and shares at lowest risk.
  3 Information systems can be used for completely new systems which were previously not possible. One example is American Airlines' Sabre booking system, a new customer service.
- Even more powerful information systems are to be expected in the future, so that there will be many more possible applications and plenty of new opportunities.
- Advances in communications technology go hand in hand with

reduced costs, as mentioned in Trend 3. But technical progress is also allowing some radical new applications, such as ISDNs (Integrated Services Digital Networks), which may revolutionize some areas of business.[24] Broadly speaking, the development of communications systems will mean not only that much more information is accessible but also that advertising and image-building will become much easier.

The effect on value potential

Just as there is value potential in technology in general (technology potential), so there is quite specific value potential in information (information potential). This includes all the possibilities offered by the use of modern information and communications systems, not just computers. It appears that progress in this area is set to continue, so information potential should become increasingly attractive for many firms.

It can safely be assumed that market potential in the information and communications sectors will continue to be attractive, but in many cases this is only really open to companies already active in the field. It is, however, true that all other companies may find their market potential increasing because of developments in information and communications, especially in the service sector, where new services can be provided.

A strong corporate or product image can represent very interesting value potential. Take, for example, the exclusive image which Zino Davidoff has successfully carried over from cigars to other high profile products such as perfumes and spirits. Here too information and communications systems have an important part to play, and as they become increasingly sophisticated so it is easier to exploit and develop image potential.

Finally we come to purchasing potential: with enhanced information and communications systems the purchasing process can be much more efficient. The marked improvements achieved by just-in-time production management are one example; the ability to check details instantly with suppliers another.

This brief summary shows how developments in information and communications systems permeate nearly all corporate functions. They affect almost every kind of value potential; in fact they can even spawn brand-new potential.

Trend 6: Significant demographic changes

By 1998 the population of the world will have grown from 5,100m. to over 6,000m. people. This growth will not be evenly spread: the populations of West Germany, Hungary and Denmark are declining, whilst in Third

World countries like Kenya and Iran the annual population growth is over 3 per cent. Generally speaking, in the highly developed industrial countries the birth rate is stagnating, whilst in the Third World the population continues to rise.

This difference in the birth rate, combined with varying life expectancy, affects the age structure of the population: there is a sharp increase in the older generation of the industrial nations, but in the Third World the younger generation is considerably more numerous. This in turn determines the structure of the working population. In many industrial nations, for instance, there are now many more women in paid employment, many of them in areas previously dominated by men.

Geographically, the company may be affected by migrations. In the EC and elsewhere (eg the USA) there are increasing moves towards the South, as witnessed by the Sophia Antipolis technology park at Valbonne near Cannes. On the other hand, Hispanic Americans are moving northwards and France is receiving immigrants from its former colonies.

The effect on value potential

With demographic developments, too, the most obvious effect is on the potential markets – the increasing importance of older consumers in industrial nations and of the Hispanic market in the USA.

No less important, however, are the effects on other potential, particularly the external human potential represented by the latent human resources of any population. Quite a few companies have already recognized the attractive value potential of old age pensioners. The Varian Corporation enables its workers to continue working on a reduced basis far beyond the usual pensionable age.[25] The considerable human potential of the female population can also be opened up by innovative employment concepts such as flexible working systems for mothers.

Trend 7: New social attitudes

Social attitudes are important to business: they influence demand in the market, and they influence the behaviour of the various stakeholders in the company – the workforce, management, shareholders, the public. Public attitudes have gone through some marked changes since the Second World War.

The current attitudes can be sketched out as follows:

- Self-development as a paramount requirement[26]
- A greater willingness to work independently, to be entrepreneurial[27]
- Increasing interest in teamwork and team activities, coupled with the desire for greater communication in the workplace[28]

- A trend away from the purely rational to intuitive behaviour.
- Greater emphasis on qualitative values.
- A growing need for freedom, often answered by part-time work.
- A new awareness, not least among consumers, of ecological concerns.
- Increasing importance of the family.[29]

There are clear advantages to be reaped by any company which can exploit these trends.

The effect on value potential

I am of the opinion that these social trends combined with the economic and demographic developments already described will have a decisive influence on value potential.

For a start, the new attitudes have an impact on human potential, with a new generation of managers and highly qualified employees. An example: for some time now several of the big banks in Europe have been trying to achieve the top position in the trading of share options, but the market leader is a small organization whose staff has an average age of 27. While many big banks suffer losses in this business, this small company is supremely profitable. How can a small firm headed by such young people manage to push many large institutions onto the defensive? The answer is simple bearing in mind current trends.

The staff of the small firm are doubtless highly qualified individualists, capable of high performance in their specialist fields – computing and mathematics. These specialists enjoy the challenge of working independently, enterprisingly and unconventionally. The small organization is best able to create a desirable working environment, thereby attracting the best-qualified candidates. The big banks are restrictive in comparison: their hours and ways of working are set down in regulations and there is a fixed salary structure, often with no allowance for productivity. Most of all there is no room for employees to share in the capital. No wonder the best young workers shy away from such rigid organizations. Progressive institutions such as the Schweizerische Kreditanstalt have recognized the problem and are doing their best to become more flexible.

This is a very common problem: everybody starts with the same strong market potential, but for above-average success the right human potential must be developed. Market potential is no longer the key. Unfortunately many firms remain blind to the fact and continue to behave as if market potential was all that mattered. They can then postpone those uncomfortable decisions that have to be made in order to develop human potential, and delay changes in their structure.

The change in attitudes, however, demands that relations between company and employees be completely rethought. It is easy for companies to open up human potential as long as they are willing to create new structures and new relationships. Companies changing in this direction will be the winners in the coming years.

The effects of changing attitudes on market potential cannot yet be precisely judged. If environmental awareness should lead to a decline in consumption, then many markets would lose their attraction. More markets are likely to become saturated and decline.

Image potential will increase as the instinctive, qualitative dimension dominates. The object of all image-building is to establish an important position by emotional means, and this will become easier as intuition takes over from rationality. A positive image can influence an individual in favour of the image holder, and images will grow in importance as long as the trend towards feelings and intuition continues.

Trend 8: Increasing concern about the environment

Public concern about the environment is increasing in the face of such issues as pollution, the greenhouse effect and the hole in the ozone layer, the dangers of nuclear technology (Chernobyl), the destruction of the rainforests and acid rain. For many committed people the most important task both now and well into the twenty-first century is to solve these ecological problems. This is bound to affect value potential.

The effect on value potential

Here again market potential is prominent. Companies already active in the right area will be able to open up attractive new markets for products which help protect the environment and conserve energy. Conversely the market potential for those companies whose activities endanger the environment is likely to suffer badly.

Huge investments in environmental protection reduce financial potential. The USA plans to spend about $20,000m. a year on improving the quality of water alone. Another $6,000m. a year is to be spent on making good soil erosion.[30]

Human potential is sure to be affected too. It will become much harder to recruit highly qualified, well educated staff in sectors which threaten the environment, while companies working towards constructive environmental solutions will find human potential opening up for them.

Trend 9: A new era in East–West relations

There have been fundamental changes in the political landscape in the USSR since Mikhail Gorbachov took office, and a new era has begun in other Eastern countries.

These countries face tremendous challenges:

- Debureaucratization and revitalization of the economy
- Modernization of production facilities; higher productivity, but also higher quality
- A massive increase in their ability to innovate
- New market structures
- Protecting the environment.

If these and many other tasks on the agenda are to be successfully tackled there will have to be much more international cooperation and trading between the different economic systems. The enormous value potential this could present is obvious. However, it is not yet certain that the necessary political reforms can be carried through in the long term, and the risk of a swing back to the hard line cannot be ruled out.

The effect on value potential

Market potential in the Eastern bloc is likely to be principally for capital goods, though there could also be expansion in consumer goods, banking and other services.

However, it seems to me that developments in Eastern Europe are opening up new kinds of potential which have more to offer than classic market potential. Direct exploitation of the market potential is likely to be very risky, so it is better to look at other methods, especially joint ventures. In 1987 and 1988, for example, the USSR entered into a total of 191 joint ventures with 33 countries, with a capital of 811m. roubles in all. Expertise can be put to good use through licensing potential. There is enormous human potential in Eastern Europe which has lain fallow till now because of bureaucracy and the prevalence of systems which inhibit self-initiative. Any company which succeeds in tapping this potential can do well.

These apparently unconventional types of potential show more promise, at least in the immediate future, than developing conventional market potential through direct sales.

Trend 10: The increasing economic importance of the Pacific Basin

Having won supremacy in the 1960s and 1970s in the field of entertainment electronics, cameras, steel and other capital goods, in the 1980s Japan succeeded in becoming the world's largest manufacturer of cars and integrated circuits, to mention only two important product areas. It was by achieving dominance in the financial sector, however, that it broke through to lead the world's economy. In 1988 eight out of the world's ten largest financial institutions, measured by market capitalization, were located in

Japan. The three largest insurance companies were also in Japan.[31] These Japanese financial companies have only limited possibilities for expansion in their own country, so of course they expand overseas.[32]

Other countries around the Pacific Rim such as Korea, Taiwan and – perhaps a little later – the People's Republic of China will also gain economic importance. These developments will inevitably have a great influence on value potential.

The effect on value potential

Increasing economic strength will give the Pacific countries new purchasing power, which will boost market potential in all kinds of areas. New financial potential is also opening up. For example, the finance used by the leveraged buyout company Kohlberg, Kravis, Roberts in the RJR–Nabisco takeover included over $5,000m. bank credit from Japan. Potential is also emerging in this trading region for joint ventures and licensing.

There will, however, be adverse effects on the current value potential of Western companies. There is the problem of increased competition. The concentrated financial power of many companies in the Far East could be increasingly used to take over companies in the West, which would mean that takeover potential for Western companies would contract. As countries in the Far East climb to the peak of world technology, so the technology potential of the West is cut down. In the 1980s Japanese motor manufacturers in the USA proved that they are also very good at making the most of (often unused) human potential. Honda and Nissan built highly productive motor factories in Ohio and Tennessee whose levels of performance and quality are among the highest in the world, far surpassing those of US manufacturers.

Conclusions for dynamic companies

Two general conclusions can be drawn from this study of the relevant future trends:

1   The coming years will provide plenty of attractive value potential for dynamic companies. In some sectors there will be interesting market potential, but potential will arise in other areas which will be just as interesting. Dynamic companies are flexible enough to make use of all kinds of potential.

2   The developments also bring dangers, as existing potential is impaired and loses its attraction. Many markets are becoming saturated. This is another reason to avoid being restricted to market potential, to keep an open mind and be alert to other, more unconventional, opportunities.

Looking at the different types of potential within the framework of emerging trends has inevitably meant a degree of overlap.

The types of value potential

As I have already observed a number of times, there is a wide variety of value potential open to development by the dynamic company. In presenting a survey of the different kinds it must be stressed that such a survey can never be complete. It is a characteristic of successful companies that they are the first to recognize and exploit unconventional value potential, before other companies start to interfere. Unfortunately any systematic study of value potential can by definition only cover potential which is already known about.

Every change in the business world affects value potential. Potential which used to be interesting loses its attraction, and new, often spectacular, potential arises. In ancient times the most interesting potential lay in taking over political office: Roman prefects, for example, became rich by imposing oppressive taxes on the people. Right up to the Renaissance robbery and extortion (holding prisoners for ransom) was a popular kind of potential, not restricted to robber barons. Fortunately times changed somewhat when in many places the state assumed the role of the tax-hungry usurper of prosperity, instead of the greedy prefects.

By contrast, changes in the business world in the last twenty years have been almost imperceptible, but none the less they have given rise to plenty of attractive new value potential. This is likely to continue in the future. At the same time old potential loses its attraction. Because of this continuous process of change, the system developed below is not a formal one, and the assessments I shall make of the attraction of value potential in the future are necessarily crude.

Value potential can lie outside the company or within it. I shall therefore distinguish between external and internal potential.

External value potential

Market potential

'Market potential is the total of possible sales in a market for a particular product (the capacity of a market).'[33] Classic management theory which perceives the company as a productive social system providing output for third parties necessarily places market potential at the centre of analysis.[34] All the company's endeavours are ultimately directed towards providing output for the sales market. Market orientation is the primary concern.[35]

Without doubt the discovery and development of rich potential markets will continue to be an important goal. However, this must become ever more difficult in this world of saturated markets and substantial overcapacity.[36] From the angle of corporate dynamism it is crucial to keep checking whether the market potential open to the company really remains sufficiently attractive. If not, then other kinds of value potential simply have to be considered.

Future promise: numerous products and their markets have reached saturation point or even entered the decline phase, while growing markets are the scene of intense competition. The attraction of market potential must therefore be on the decline for many companies. One remaining possibility is a partial switch to market niches.

Financial potential

Financial potential embraces all the possibilities of financial transactions with outsiders.

Nowadays innovative financial management goes far beyond simply procuring outside capital and managing financial assets. Its aim must be to seize the opportunities arising from the globalization of the world markets, deregulation (Europe 1992) and other, similar, developments. The high rate of innovation in financial services and the increasing spread of information point to a rise in the attraction of financial potential.

Future promise: growing.

Information potential

Information potential comprises all the benefits that can be generated by the use of modern information and communications systems.

Progress in microtechnology and related areas will create great openings for dynamic companies as long as they are able to make innovative and conceptual use of these opportunities (the strategic application of information science).

Future promise: high.

Procurement potential

Procurement potential includes all the ways a company can increase value by purchasing skilfully and setting up effective systems.

Procurement potential is likely to become more attractive because of trends such as globalization, improved East–West relations, and European integration, as well as technological developments, for example the information systems which have made just-in-time production possible.

Future promise: growing.

External human potential

(External) human potential denotes the unused human resources in any population.

There is still a plentiful supply of human resources waiting to be tapped in both West and East. Personnel management leaves a lot to be desired, as managers in general pay too little attention to human needs, and new social attitudes call for a shift in the relationship between company and workforce. Political (East–West) and demographic developments are opening up many new opportunities, too.

Future promise: very high.

Takeover and restructuring potential

By takeover and restructuring potential I mean the chances a company has to acquire and – as a rule – restructure other companies.

The wave of takeovers in the second half of the 1980s raised prices so high that in some countries the relevant potential has been sharply reduced. Besides, many companies have now dismantled their top-heavy management structures and reorganized, so that the number of 'undermanaged companies' is decreasing. There are still some openings in countries like Switzerland and West Germany, where legal restrictions make reorganization difficult, and, in sectors which are stagnating or withering away, companies will be forced to merge.

Future promise: medium to diminishing.

Cooperation potential

Cooperation potential means possibilities for joint ventures and other forms of cooperation.

The opening up of world markets and better international relations, as well as technological necessity (such as the escalation of development costs), mean that increased cooperation is essential. Dividing the company up into organizational units and working together in joint ventures will also tie in with the growing desire of employees for more independence and less complicated structures.

Future promise: growing.

Regulation potential

Regulation potential means the opportunities available to a company to improve its profitability by influencing legislation or exploiting new or existing laws, regulations and official standards.

Although frequent attempts at protectionism, regulation, subvention and so on are made in many countries, this potential is rather limited. During the 1980s the advantages of deregulation have been demonstrated in a number of countries, while the problems of the Communist bloc reveal the limitations of planning and intervention.

Future promise: medium.

Internal value potential

Cost-cutting potential

Cost-cutting potential is represented by the cost savings a company may be able to make.

Cost-cutting potential exists in companies which have not adequately rationalized their production processes or have gone the wrong way about it. They may be making insufficient use of modern equipment such as automatic machinery, or they may still be suffering from overorganization and too many staff at headquarters. There is still much cost-cutting to do in this respect, especially in the public sector, but many Western companies have already taken steps in the right direction.

Future promise: medium.

Expertise potential

Expertise potential embraces all the possibilities open to a company of using its own knowledge. This could be knowledge protected by law (patents) or unprotected specialist expertise in the company's activities.

Many companies have accumulated a high level of knowledge about product technology and innovation, or even marketing, production, procurement, information and so on. There is so much innovation at present that there would appear to be a great deal of expertise potential in very many companies, and this is often underused.

Future promise: medium to high.

Synergy potential

Synergy potential is present in existing structures which could be used for additional activities.

Just as companies are full of expertise potential, so many of them have structures which could be used for new activities. These could include existing production plant, distribution channels, marketing organizations or purchasing organizations. A company can often take advantage of the trends described above by synergic use of existing structures. The more changes occur, the greater this potential becomes.

Future promise: available.

Organizational potential

By organizational potential we mean the opportunities to increase productivity by rearranging processes and structures.

It is widely recognized nowadays that bureaucracies are not best placed to generate maximum productivity. Their great drawback is that they cannot adapt to new developments. The more circumstances change, the greater the discrepancy between the actual productivity of the organization and what it could achieve.

Organizational potential can be exploited by, for example, breaking the company up into small units under a holding structure. Innovations in the organization of processes can lead to great improvements, as we saw in the case of Glaxo, at the beginning of the book. Using organizational means to minimize the time needed to introduce products, production run times and so on is also becoming much more important.

Future promise: great (especially for medium and larger companies).

Internal human potential

(Internal) human potential is all the human resources available within the company which are not being used.

As with external human potential, internal human resources in many companies are still underutilized. Demotivation and lethargy are widespread. If people are given a sense of purpose, vision and motivation, astonishing forces can be released. Here too the change in attitudes needs to be taken into account. Many companies have not woken up to the fact that today's employees think quite differently to their predecessors just a few years ago, let alone decades ago, and so have not changed accordingly. There is still considerable potential here.

Future promise: high.

Balance sheet potential

Balance sheet potential is all the possibilities open to a company to redeploy its assets or liabilities to better effect.

As we have seen there is likely to be continued economic turbulence, expressed by swings in the rates of exchange, inflation, interest and so on. These have already led to some discrepancies between a company's value on paper and in real terms. The sharp rise in property values in many countries at the end of the 1980s, for instance, has meant that some companies could achieve much higher profits by redeploying some of their assets (selling, reletting and so on). This is the kind of potential which attracts raiders.

In principle there is balance sheet potential in assets and liabilities. On the asset side both current and fixed assets can be optimized, while on the liabilities side it is important that the company is being financed in the most effective way.

It is important, however, not to launch blindly into asset-stripping, but to take a long-term view.

Future promise: high.

Figure 2.4 gives an overview of the different types of value potential available in the late twentieth century.

Value potential	
External value potential	*Internal value potential*
Market potential	Cost-cutting potential
Financial potential	Expertise potential
Information potential	Synergy potential
Procurement potential	Organizational potential
External human potential	Internal human potential
Takeover and restructuring potential	Balance sheet potential
Cooperation potential	etc.
(Regulation potential)	
etc.	

Figure 2.4 *The different types of value potential*

The innovative approach to value potential

As we have seen, attractive value potential is nearly always some new combination of circumstances resulting from a change in the business environment. To exploit this new situation the dynamic company almost always has to adapt its product, and this entails being creative and innovative.

This is borne out in my analysis of dynamic companies. Behind their dynamism there is always innovation, albeit at different levels. Let us look at some examples.

The dynamic expansion of Club Méditerranée started with the innovation of the club village. This concept, developed in the 1950s, represents an innovation in many respects compared with the other holidays on offer at that time: everything – accommodation, sophisticated cuisine, organized activities, evening entertainment – is included in the price. While on holiday the guest only has to pay for drinks at the bar (with special club money). The carefree atmosphere to which this contributes is encouraged by many other innovations, including the entertainment laid on every evening by the GOs (*gentils organisateurs*, Club Med's popular couriers). In short, the success of Club Méditerranée can be directly attributed to the highly innovative product with which it tapped very precisely the potential of holidaymakers looking for a carefree holiday.

Innovation is always at the centre of dynamic expansion, but it does not always involve the product. The dynamic expansion of Bertelsmann in the 1960s, for instance, could scarcely have taken place without a sizeable financial input. Richard Mohn, the head of the company, had to open up additional financial potential. He developed a participation model, by which the employees could have a share in the capital of their company. The model was unique at the time and represented not only a financial innovation but a new, motivating approach to employee relations. I shall be discussing this innovation in greater detail in Chapter 6.

The example of Bertelsmann shows that you must also innovate in order to exploit internal potential, and this is true whether it be cost-cutting, reorganization or transfer of expertise. This must be why so many companies find difficulty in exploiting their internal potential, for innovation is generally very risky, and the management of many companies is simply not prepared to take risks.

What constitutes an innovation? Strictly speaking, to be innovative an activity must be completely new of its kind, so that no company has yet put it into practice.[37] In the dynamic context, however, that definition is too narrow. What is important is that the activities should be new to the field in which they are to be applied. The cash-and-carry concept of Metro-

Markt was not a true innovation, since stores of this kind already existed by the end of the 1950s in the USA and in West Germany, Terfloh and Snoek having opened the first German cash-and-carry store in Bochum in 1957. Metro-Markt's concept was somewhat different to that, particularly in its pioneering use of information technology, but the real innovation lay in opening up the concept to other user groups, such as the inhabitants of Mühlheim and its environs, for whom the whole idea was new. Metro-Markt offered them great advantages over their existing suppliers: lower prices, wider ranges and longer opening hours. The same is true of financial innovations. The firm of Arden, based in Zug, took over the concept of leveraged buyouts which was originally developed in the USA, and has been using it successfully in Europe since 1982. The secret of its success is that the concept was new to the takeover targets; it makes no difference who actually invented leveraged buyouts.

Guidelines for management

The basic requirement

Dynamic managers recognize and develop attractive value potential. This can lie outside the company or within it.

Origins

Uncertainties resulting from changes in the business environment frequently give rise to new value potential and reduce the attraction of familiar potential. Therefore dynamic managers are constantly aware of the main trends and anticipate their possible effects on value potential.

Phases of value potential

Value potential goes through four phases, beginning with emergence, through growth and maturity to decline. Dynamic managers concentrate wherever possible on potential in its emerging or growth phase.

Overcoming mind set

The conventional businessman sticks to the tramline thinking of market and technological potential, ignoring the attractive value potential of other areas of business which can often be found in established industrial companies and in changing circumstances. By contrast the dynamic manager makes creative and unprejudiced use of the chances which present themselves.

Innovation

As a rule newly emerging potential can only be harnessed by new kinds of business activity. The dynamic manager has the strength to carry through the necessary innovations.

Notes

1   See Ulrich, 1970, pp. 153–5.
2   See Porter, 1980; Pümpin, 1981a; Abell, 1980; Lorange, 1977; Gälweiler, 1987; Hinterhuber, 1984; Kirsch and Roventa, 1983, especially the article by Kirsch and Trux, pp. 43–63. Pleitner examines the factors of excellence for small and medium-sized companies in Pleitner, 1988, pp. 14–25.
3   See Porter, 1987, pp. 43–59.
4   See Pümpin, 1989.
5   See Hamilton, 1988, pp. 46–51.
6   See eg Freudenmann, p. 8; Schelker, 1976, p. 59.
7   See Greiner, 1982, pp. 7–15.
8   Names have been changed to protect confidentiality.
9   See Naisbitt, 1984, pp. 159 ff.
10 The following publications were used: Merrian and Makover, 1988 and Naisbitt, 1984.
11 See *Wall Street Journal*, 1987.
12 See Tapie, 1986.
13 See Winteler, 1988, p. 31.
14 See for example Ohmae, 1985, pp. 35 ff.; Levitt, 1983a, pp. 92 ff., and 1983b, pp. 20–49; Casson, 1984, pp. 215–376.
15 See Finneran, 1986, pp. 9 ff.
16 See Percy and McMinn, 1988, F2.
17 See Kirkland, 1988, pp. 121 ff.
18 See Mayo, 1987, pp. 499 ff.
19 Ibid.
20 See Suplee, 1986.
21 See Amato, 1988.
22 See eg Robertson, Achilladelis, Jervis, 1972.
23 See Peters, 1987.
24 See Mayo, op. cit.
25 See Ramirez, 1989, pp. 107 ff.
26 See Maccoby, 1988, pp. 50 ff.
27 See Cetron, 1988, pp. 29 ff.
28 Ibid.

29 See Fowles, 1988, F3.
30 See Myers, 1988, pp. 190 ff.
31 See Turner, 1987, pp. 11 ff.
32 Ibid.
33 Meffert, 1977, p. 186. Weinhold differentiates between the concepts of market capacity and market potential as follows: The market capacity is the (physical) ability of the market to absorb, calculated from the number of people in need of the product and the average rate of use. Market potential also takes account of purchasing power and the price. See Weinhold, 1988, pp. 75 and 79.
34 Wehrli, 1980, p. 63.
35 See Peters and Waterman, 1982, pp. 156 ff. 292 ff.
36 See Belz, 1989, pp. 34 ff., 187 ff.
37 Innovation is defined in the *Management Enzyklopädie* 'as the creation and execution of changes of an innovative nature.... They (technological innovations) appear as new products or product generations, new software, new systems or new production methods'.

Chapter 3

Multiplication: the path to effective expansion

What does multiplication mean?

Multiplication is the second of the three cornerstones of business dynamics. Why is it so important?

Imagine a company which is lucky enough to make a highly lucrative acquisition. This one takeover will get the company moving but after a while it will lose impetus and grind to a halt again. To keep moving it must make more profitable takeovers.

In other words, it takes more than a one-off transaction to sustain corporate dynamism: it takes a complete concept. The key to building a concept is to repeat an activity which exploits value potential. This systematic repetition is what we are calling multiplication.

It follows that the targeted value potential must be so great that it is possible to carry out the relevant business activity more than once. Only value potential which allows frequent repetition of the activity which harnesses it is really attractive.

This may appear to be stating the obvious. After all, no market strategist would develop a product – except perhaps on a large-scale project – for which there was only limited market potential. One of the first questions always asked is about the size of the expected market. And yet firms repeatedly fail to multiply, even though they could have reached a sizeable market and therefore great value potential.

For example, in the 1960s, as we have already seen, Metro was the only company to apply the principle of multiplication to the cash-and-carry business in West Germany. Its various rivals in the field failed to multiply and Metro came to dominate self-service wholesaling in the Federal Republic. While it developed in the most dynamic way, some of the competition stagnated and finally had to stop trading.

When potential has nothing to do with the market, there is even less multiplication. Surprisingly few firms think of multiplying activities which are not sales-related. I think the reason for this lies in the discipline of accountancy, where acquisitions, financial transactions and so on are seen as extraordinary activities. The term 'extraordinary items' emphasizes that activities of this kind are in no way to be considered ordinary business.[1] Once again the standards which have evolved in theory and practice over decades have led to a mind set which stands in the way of the dynamic exploitation of innovative value potential. Imaginative, dynamic companies, on the other hand, turn extraordinary items into the mainstay of their business!

Why is there too little multiplication?

Overemphasis on diversification

There are conflicting pressures on companies. The customers want the product to be adapted as far as possible to their individual needs, and as these needs become ever more diverse, attempts are made to make the product more and more individualized. This pressure is reinforced by the sales and marketing departments, and it is not surprising that in many companies the management gives in to it and fragments the product line by arbitrarily extending the range.

Cost-efficiency pushes in the opposite direction. The best way to reduce costs is to manufacture and market goods in the greatest possible quantities – in other words, to multiply. This is true not only of market-oriented activities, but of anything which aims to tap value potential. So there is always a conflict between 'laissez-faire' diversification and multiplication.[2]

In my opinion many companies nowadays are bowing too much to extreme diversification instead of consistent multiplication. Dynamic companies put all their weight into multiplication, once they have identified promising value potential. Let's take some examples.

In the early 1970s, Metro decided to introduce the cash-and-carry stores which were so successful in West Germany into France. To save time and on cost grounds they decided to stay with the layout which had been proven in West Germany, although they knew that a different layout would have been more suitable for the French, with their different needs. For example, they earmarked quite a large area for frozen food, despite the fact that the French market for these products was not nearly so well developed as the German. The advantages of rapid multiplication outweighed the disadvantages of insufficient diversification: Metro was quickly established on the best sites, and it was easy enough to adjust later to specific needs.

This example illustrates that it is the *relative* benefit of the activity to be multiplied that matters. It must offer genuine advantages over the current activity, but it does not have to be absolutely perfect from the very beginning. In the Metro example, the (multiplied) Metro markets were an important innovation compared with the conventional distribution outlets of the time. They were better for the customers and so the customers preferred them even in their imperfect state. Even multiplying a system which was not yet perfect was successful. Excessive perfectionism is the enemy of multiplication, and hence of dynamism.

This concept of multiplying rapidly first and improving later contrasts somewhat with the excellence approach. Peters and Waterman use the motto 'close to the customer' to encourage the company to orient itself firmly towards customer demand. Diversification is given a prominent role.[3] Dynamic companies act differently. They want their products to be that little bit better, but once that little bit has been achieved they multiply intensively rather than perfecting the product further. The difference between the Peters and Waterman approach and this one can be put down to value potential. A company which is set on surviving in a saturated market with shrinking potential has no choice but to diversify and be extremely customer-oriented. If it finds promising value potential, however, it can multiply instead of diversifying.

Personal factors

In many cases a company fails to multiply because its owners do not want to expand. Every proprietor has the right to feel like this, and there can be no real objection.

Often, however, the shareholders or other stakeholders want the company to be more dynamic. The top management may claim to be in favour of expansion but simply fails to do anything about it, for a number of basic reasons. Habit is very difficult to overcome, for one thing. Let's take an example:

An architect had built up a very sound practice in his local region, with over fifty employees. During this build-up phase he took the role of head salesman, securing new contracts, and chief designer. He would draft rough designs in consultation with the clients and pass them on to his employees for the detailed work.

Expanding by multiplying – eg by opening new branches – would have meant working in a completely different way. This strategy would have been unwelcome for some very concrete reasons:

- The architect felt secure acquiring the contracts and preparing the rough drafts. Expanding would have meant he had to give up these familiar activities and replace them with unfamiliar ones.
- The architect had developed good personal relationships with the clients in his local market. If the practice had expanded he would no longer have been able to nurture these relationships, since his time would have been taken up primarily with opening and overseeing the new branches.
- Expansion inevitably involves taking risks, something the architect was not prepared to do.

This is a clear example of the various reasons why heads of companies may be unwilling to expand. Complacency, habit, personal relationships, an aversion to risks, all play an important role.

The effects of multiplication

Why is multiplication so important to corporate dynamism? The main reason lies in the host of beneficial effects it has on the dynamic process.

Multiplication means concentration of forces

Multiplication ties in with one of the central strategic principles: it inevitably means concentrating forces. This is because, every time an activity which exploits value potential is repeated, all the resources available to the company are concentrated on the chosen potential. They cannot be wasted on other activities.

The story of Body Shop is a good example of this principle. In the 1970s Body Shop developed a new concept in cosmetics which appealed to the growing number of consumers who were interested in natural products and environmentally aware. Here was value potential with great promise. Body Shop immediately began to multiply the new shops it had developed, opening no fewer than 360, largely identical, shops in the space of twelve years. The potential was so great that the question of diversification simply didn't arise: resources and time could all be concentrated on expanding the chain of shops. This wholehearted concentration of forces brought great success for the company. Between 1986 and 1988 turnover increased from £17.4m. to £46.2m. Today the company has nearly 3,000 employees all over the world. In 1984 it successfully went public. Trading started at 11.6 pence, and by 1988 share prices had reached £5.64.

Multiplication means simplicity

The importance of simplicity to successful business is constantly underestimated. In today's complex world even relatively straightforward tasks can be very demanding. Take a small, single-product firm. Someone in the company has to be able to complete the various official forms and be familiar with the ever more complicated laws and regulations. Modern technical aids, such as PCs and NC machines, have to be used. The customers' different demands have to be met. The list could go on for ever. Managing even a small, straightforward concern like this is quite a challenge.

What happens if our single-product entrepreneur decides to introduce a new line? Now he will probably have to install new machinery and master a new production process. He has to consider any legal requirements for the new product. Perhaps he will be supplying new customers, with totally different demands, and buying new raw materials. There must be more coordination, so as to exploit possible synergies. With every new business activity the complexity of the company increases disproportionately – the costs of complexity rise exponentially.

At the other end of the scale is simplicity. Repeating similar activities brings a number of advantages: low coordination costs, greater familiarity with the repeated activity, easier communication among the staff, to name but a few.

Multiplication helps to keep complexity under control. This is extremely important for dynamic growth: the motivation to expand is much greater when similar activities are multiplied than when many different activities are developed, just because it is so much simpler. In the latter case there is always the danger of losing impetus because of inexperience, risks which are difficult to assess or the high cost of coordination.

Multiplication means greater cost-efficiency

The learning curve which comes from multiplication is extremely important to dynamic development. In the 1960s Henderson conducted empirical researches which indicated that unit costs could be reduced by as much as 20–30 per cent by doubling the cumulative quantity.[4] Of course production quantities must depend on the market capacity the company can command. These reductions in costs thanks to the so-called learning curve can be attributed to a number of factors.

Basically, as output increases the whole organization goes through a learning process which leads to greater efficiency: better use is made of raw materials, production processes are rationalized, warehousing is greatly improved. The marketing department finds out the best way to advertise and how to get the best results from its budget. The personnel department is able to smooth out its administrative processes, and personnel selection can be improved.

The learning curve can be exploited in all the activities involved in developing value potential. Opening a new franchise becomes ever more efficient as experience increases. The same is true of innovation.

The knowledge gained in a learning curve is a well-known feature which is already taken into account in competitive strategies. But competitive strategies are always geared to products sold in existing markets. They emphasize the reduction of unit costs, but underestimate the huge advantages the learning curve can bring to other activities.

For example: thanks to the learning curve, unit costs can be reduced by 25 per cent on average by doubling the cumulative quantity. If the quantity is doubled (by multiplication) four times over (ie sixteen times the original quantity), it is possible to reduce unit costs to 37.3 per cent of the original costs. There are two important points here. Firstly, with skilful multiplication the activity can quite quickly be doubled four times over. Secondly, the benefits of this multiplication are enormous: our calculation shows a reduction in unit costs of over sixty per cent.

In the mid-1970s the managers of a medium-sized industrial company decided to try cooperation as a way to reach new markets. Their first attempt was extremely difficult, requiring lengthy negotiations before the agreements could be signed. Some projects had to be given up altogether. But in time the experience they had gained began to pay off for they now knew how the cooperation deal should work, and how to negotiate. After a relatively short time they had attained such professionalism that they were able to put their plans into action very quickly and at a fraction of the original costs.

The differences between a company which has entered into cooperation only once and a company which repeatedly enters into such agreements are plain to see. The latter will be far more efficient. But this fact is largely ignored. How many companies think of the effects of multiplication on cooperation, acquisition, reorganization, analyses of overheads or the exploitation of expertise? Activities like these are still generally seen as extraordinary events which occur only once in the life of a firm, or at any rate only sporadically.

Multiplication saves time

Partly because of the learning curve, multiplication can save time. Repetition of a task leads to greater proficiency at it, saving time in several ways:

• Workers learn to carry out the task more quickly as their skills improve.

- Thanks to these increased skills, there are fewer mistakes and problems, and so fewer corrections have to be made.
- This means that less time has to be spent on quality control.

Again, the amount of time that can be saved can be considerable. In the course of its many acquisitions Hanson plc gained so much knowledge and ability, for example, that in 1986 it managed to make the £2,500m. acquisition of Imperial Tobacco in less than seven days. Other, less experienced, firms take far more time, even for much smaller acquisitions.

Multiplication helps to shape a corporate concept

As Peters and Waterman and many other authors have pointed out,[5] successful firms generally have a consistent, clear and communicable corporate concept. Multiplication is the ultimate expression of such a concept, for multiplying a single business activity makes a company extremely consistent. Look at the example of Hilti AG, a company based in Schaan, in Liechtenstein, which produces fastening systems for the construction industry. Its success is largely due to the high quality of customer service it is able to offer through its ingenious direct sales system. By multiplying this system Hilti has created a strong corporate concept, with all its attendant advantages. Another example is the world's largest cement manufacturer, the Holderbank Group, whose preeminent position is built on the multiplication of cement factories. The corporate concept of restructurers such as Hanson is expressed, not in products or branches, but in their systematic and highly professional acquisition and reorganization processes.

Companies which multiply sensibly automatically develop an appropriate corporate concept, with beneficial effects which should not at any cost be underestimated. To exploit value potential on an *ad hoc* basis is to forgo great advantages.

Figure 3.1 gives an overview of the many effects of multiplication.

The result: multiplication generates momentum

Multiplication always has a dynamic effect. At best it can create an escalating spiral of growth so that the company's own momentum carries it forward. Management and workers on a learning curve soon realize that they keep getting better at the activities they are multiplying, which raises the value generated for the stakeholders. This in turn stimulates the employees to exploit the value potential even more. Similarly, time saved

Multiplication means *concentration of forces*
Multiplication means *simplicity*
Multiplication means *cost-efficiency*
Multiplication means *time savings*
Multiplication means *a strong corporate concept*

Figure 3.1 *The effects of multiplication*

by multiplication can be used for further multiplication.

As tasks and processes become easier to understand, the risks are reduced and there is greater willingness to extend. Concentration of forces allows the major problems to be more deeply analysed and better understood, so that there is greater certainty about the way ahead and higher motivation for further expansion.

A strong corporate concept based on multiplication makes it clear to everyone which way the company is heading, and the entire workforce can push towards the same goals.

So multiplication is a vital cornerstone of business dynamics, but one which has been sadly underestimated by too many companies.

The forms of multiplication

When a company is to be energized by multiplication the first question is what exactly should be multiplied. This question brings us to the forms of multiplication. They fall into two basic types: multiplication of processes and multiplication of systems.[6]

Both types apply to practically every kind of value potential. In process multiplication complete processes, such as the procurement process or financing, are repeated many times. In system multiplication whole systems, such as distribution outlets or factories, are reproduced complete with all their component parts.

Multiplication of processes

What processes can be multiplied to develop value potential?

- *Products and production processes.* The most common form of multiplication is to produce and market a product in the largest possible quantity. Not only the product is multiplied, but also production processes, if a new product line is introduced, and marketing processes, to break into new markets. Sony successfully multiplied its product Walkman. Before the Walkman was introduced in 1979 Sony planned sales of 60,000. When it came onto the market in July of that year demand was so great that Sony was forced to double production after only four months. The fruits of this multiplication were fantastic: 602,000 Walkmen were sold in 1980 and over 2 million in 1981. In 1988 the sales figures were around 11.1 million. This overwhelming success took Sony so much by surprise that plans to introduce a different name had to be abandoned because the Walkman was already so firmly established.

- *Marketing processes.* To exploit the vast potential of the cosmetics market the American firm Mary Kay Cosmetics developed its own sales procedure, which specified exactly how Mary Kay's products were to be presented and sold door-to-door. The 'beauty consultants' (saleswomen) were intensively trained in the sales procedure. Later Mary Kay multiplied this process, setting up a sales force over the whole of the United States. This consistent multiplication is one of the main factors of Mary Kay's success.

- *Advertising processes.* Every experienced consumer goods firm multiplies advertising processes as a matter of course. One good example is Esso's famous tiger advertisements, which appeared almost all over the world.

- *R&D processes.* The multiplication of R&D is still comparatively rare. Porsche carries out research not only for itself but also for others and thus multiplies the use of its research process.

- *Innovation processes.* Innovation is wider than R&D, involving the whole development and introduction of a product. One firm which has acquired real mastery of innovation is 3M. The outstanding methods of innovation which it has developed to harness technological and market potential are skilfully applied in all 49 of its operational divisions.

- *Financial processes.* Some firms have multiplied and hence professionalized the process of fund-raising. This is the case with venture capital companies such as Advent or APA, Alan Patrickof Associates. The latter has built up venture capital funds in Britain, France and the USA amounting to a total of over $500m.

- *Motivation processes.* Great value potential can be tapped in many firms by releasing the creative and productive energy of the workforce. The processes which achieve this can be multiplied, in just the same way as all the other processes. Hewlett-Packard has developed a comprehensive package for human resource management. Offices, conference rooms and canteens in all its establishments follow a uniform layout designed to encourage communication, and other motivation programmes have been instigated worldwide.

- *Acquisition processes.* Forbo AG of Switzerland has become one of the leading European companies in floor and wall coverings. One of the main planks of its strategy was taking over small, local manufacturers. The experience it gained by this multiple application of the acquisition process soon enabled it to integrate firms very quickly, and this contributed greatly to its success.

- *Restructuring processes.* Acquiring and restructuring other companies is the core strategy of various firms, such as Chargeur SA in France, or, in Britain, Hanson plc and BTR, where Chairman Sir David Owen practises the strategy. These firms make skilful and repeated use of their knowledge and the associated processes.

This list shows the multitude of processes which can be multiplied, and illustrates how successful companies exploit these opportunities to achieve dominance.

Multiplication of systems

It is not only individual elements or processes which can be multiplied in order to harness value potential, but complete systems as well. By a system we mean a physical, relatively autonomous organization consisting of hardware as well as software elements. It will probably be geographically isolated from the rest of the organization. System multiplication has become widespread in the second half of the twentieth century. Here again I should like to describe some of the main forms:

- *Retail outlets.* Sales units, with benefits for the sales partner, are set up close to the customers. The ubiquitous Benetton shops are well known, as is Bally–Arola. In every case a specific system is designed and multiplied. The system consists of goods, display, shop fittings, the service system, the reporting system – in Benetton even the pop music. Retail outlets are multiplied in a wide range of retail sectors from McDonald's restaurants, photography shops such as Photo Porst, cosmetics shops such as Yves Rocher and Body Shop, chemists such as Dropa, the Aldi discount stores, to Marks & Spencer's department stores and the Wal-Mart Stores which are so successful in the USA. I have deliberately made no distinction here between chain stores and franchises, since both represent a multiplication of the system. From the motivational point of view, however, there is a fundamental difference. Franchises as a rule exploit both market and human potential, satisfying the desire of many people nowadays to run their own businesses. This phenomenon will be discussed in more detail later.
- *Marketing organizations.* In the course of expansion many firms have built up international marketing organizations, generally consisting

of national headquarters with regional outlets. Where every national company is seen as an integral unit, this too is system multiplication.

- *Distribution centres.* Physical distribution has become very important of late. The establishment of distribution centres or complete distribution organizations represents another form of system multiplication.
- *Production plant.* The multiplication of production plant involves building or buying many regional production facilities, often worldwide. The Swiss Holderbank Group has consistently followed this policy and in 1987 had 68 cement works in 22 countries.

System multiplication has always been a key feature of expansive management. It was even used successfully by the Fuggers, the fifteenth-century merchants from Augsburg who established trading posts in all the important Hanseatic ports and elsewhere. In the nineteenth and twentieth centuries practically all multinational firms multiplied their marketing organizations in a similar way.

The problem now for many multinationals is that they finished setting up subsidiaries in most of the relevant foreign markets around the time of the Second World War. In other words, the value potential of system multiplication is widely exhausted, which cripples the dynamic forces of those companies which are unwilling to look for promising new value potential and develop it by multiplication.

The forms of multiplication are shown in Figure 3.2.

Forms of multiplication

Multiplication of processes	*Multiplication of systems*
Production processes	Retail outlets
Marketing processes	Marketing organizations
Advertising processes	Distribution centres
R&D processes	Production plant
Innovation processes	etc.
Financial processes	
Motivation processes	
Acquisition processes	
Restructuring processes	

Figure 3.2 *The forms of multiplication*

Judging the forms of multiplication

Any value potential can be exploited in the shape of individual elements or processes or complete systems, and the summaries above have shown which of these most lend themselves to multiplication. For many firms the question will be which form of multiplication will be most appropriate to their dynamic development. Some concrete rules can be sketched out here.

While the multiplication of single elements can give good results, greater success usually comes from multiplying integral processes or systems. The more each process or system contains, the higher the chances of success. Hanson's restructuring processes are integral, for every restructuring necessarily involves everything to do with the company in question. Multiplying a simple business function, say, a single sales process, has less to recommend it.

The same goes for system multiplication. There is more promise in multiplying a broad-based unit such as a Metro cash-and-carry store than in multiplying a simple distribution outlet for paint.

In spite of this, many companies even now restrict themselves to multiplying elements or at best simple processes. These companies increasingly find themselves up against the limits imposed by saturated markets. The answer may be to change from element or process multiplication to system multiplication. For example: the West German firm of Plastic AG[7] produced plastic parts for delivery to car manufacturers in Europe, the USA and the Far East, and exports made up 70 per cent of its total output. In the mid-1980s the company needed to extend its production facilities, but it was doubtful whether the extension would be viable in view of the prices that could be obtained and the high costs of freight. The problem was resolved by turning to system multiplication. Small, flexible production units were built in a franchise system close to the motor manufacturers. Production conditions were better and the motor manufacturers were happier, as communications were easier, deliveries were faster and more flexible, and there were altogether fewer problems. Success was clinched by the latent potential which was harnessed in the form of young entrepreneurs eager to set up their own independent business with the help of the carefully worked-out franchise system.

In my opinion, therefore, the search should be on for possible system multiplication, for it is this area which holds the greatest potential.

Multiplication in practice

At first glance multiplication appears to be quite a simple undertaking. All it involves is applying processes or systems as often as possible. If an innovative product is to be produced and sold in the largest possible quantities, then the highest possible product figures must be established and maintained. Where a method of acquisition or reorganization has been developed, it should simply be applied wherever it can be. Systems, say, an IKEA furniture store on a greenfield site, should be reproduced as many times as possible.

But, as every practitioner knows, it's the details that are tricky. Thus Dr Hereth of Metro AG on the multiplication of Metro SB wholesale stores in Italy: 'Our expansion in Italy was reminiscent of *Don Camillo and Peppone*! Because of a strike we couldn't register the company in time. Our rivals found out and made sure the shop was closed just before Christmas – at the height of the season. We were involved in a full-scale cloak and dagger operation to open the market again. We had to be very creative.'

Similar stories cropped up in all the firms we talked to. Again and again it appears that for every action they took to multiply they were faced with a horde of obstacles. But this experience is invaluable for dynamic development.

Some courses of action have been tried and tested:

- Pursuing a policy of linear expansion, in which multiplication follows a certain rhythm. Bertelsmann and Jacobs Suchard both deliberately follow a rhythmic progression; in fact Bertelsmann has a set cycle of major acquisitions. Taking over companies too often would make it difficult to integrate them, while too few takeovers would lead to a loss of impetus.
- Developing defence tactics to keep the flank free for expansion. If multiplication is to happen quickly then any disruptive influences have to be identified at an early stage and an action plan must be made to avoid the disruption.
- Working out highly creative solutions to overcome the obstacles. All dynamic companies cause changes, and there will always be groups who try to hinder change because it harms their interests. Specialist and lay critics will object particularly where internal value potential is involved, such as redeploying assets to exploit balance sheet potential. Creative solutions have an important part to play in overcoming these problems.
- Constantly ensuring that key managers are highly motivated. The setbacks with which any expansionist activity is fraught are naturally demotivating, and it is important that energy should be put into driving the plan forward undamaged.
- Exploiting all the advantages of multiplication, particularly the benefits of the learning curve. The effects of multiplication do not occur automatically.

Speed is crucial to success in the growth phase, for two reasons:

1   Some strategic activities can only be instigated at quite specific times, what Abell calls 'strategic windows'.[8] Abell recommends that opportunities should be seized as quickly as possible, as soon as the strategic window opens. Otherwise competitors may get there first and 'close the window'.
2   It is important to generate and take advantage of impetus within the company. The corporate culture must encourage rapid action and time saving.

Naturally there will be difficulties throughout the company in the course of multiplication. New employees have to be integrated and educated in the corporate culture of the dynamic company. Capacity has to be extended constantly, which introduces the problem of financing. A balance must be maintained between internal and external capital. Leaning too hard on internal capital slows down expansion and means giving up dominant positions, while expanding too quickly can lead to a liquidity problem and loss of independence.

The limits of multiplication

In an ideal world value potential would allow virtually unlimited multiplication. There are cases like this in real life. American Express sees no limit to the charge card business, and McDonald's feels that the market potential for fast food is still far from exhausted.

However, in many cases there are strict limits on the possibilities for multiplication. Some value potential is found in a precisely defined number of targets – acquisition potential in particular. The food industry, for example, could hardly become any more concentrated: there are scarcely any companies left to acquire.

Multiplication of internal potential is inherently limited, especially in medium-sized and smaller firms. A cost-cutting programme in a company with three profit centres can after all only be multiplied by three.

Value potential which allows only a few transactions may certainly be worth developing, but will often produce only isolated impulses rather than a sustained drive. In applying the principle of dynamism, therefore, it is important to consider how much multiplication is possible with the given value potential, especially where internal potential is involved.

Guidelines for management

Multiplication as a basis for expansion

Only the multiplication of business activities allows the dynamic entrepreneur and manager to take his company into new dimensions. It is this which sets him apart from the manager aiming at one great transaction, or the static manager, barren of ideas, who simply protects the status quo.

Effects

Multiplication means concentration of forces, simplicity, the cost-efficiency and time savings associated with a learning curve. It releases expansionist forces and helps to build a corporate concept. The entrepreneurial manager makes the most of all these effects.

Multiplication that pays

The dynamic manager tries above all to multiply sophisticated processes or integral systems. The more comprehensive the system the greater the benefits.

Starting to multiply

As soon as the activity to be multiplied offers concrete advantages over the alternatives, multiplication takes precedence over perfectionism.

Rapid, consistent multiplication

The dynamic manager puts multiplication into practice as fast and as powerfully as possible.

Notes

1 See Siegwart, Caytas and Mahari, 1988a, p. 44.
2 See Borner, 1984, pp. 18ff.
3 See Peters and Waterman, 1982, pp. 156 ff. Peters and Waterman talk about tailoring to the customers' requirements. A company's market is divided into segments until specific products and services can be tailored to them. Ibid, p. 182.
4 See Henderson, 1974, p. 19.

5 See Peters and Waterman, 1982, pp. 308ff., 314, 316; Pümpin, 1989.
6 Theoretically element multiplication should be added here, in which for example a product or an advertising brochure is multiplied. However all elements are produced in processes, so we have preferred to consider processes here.
7 At the request of the company concerned the name used here is fictional.
8 See Abell, 1980, pp. 223–7.

Chapter 4

Growth promoters: vehicles of dynamism

Why growth promoters?

The third cornerstone of corporate dynamism is the presence of one or more entrepreneurial people, who initiate the dynamics and stimulate the management of the company. They are the true promoters of growth.

Growth promoters can appear in any position in the company, eg:

- Owner–manager
- Non-executive member or chairman of the board
- Managing director or executive director
- Departmental head
- Member of middle or lower management

Their common feature is that they are not purely administrators or technocrats, but active entrepreneurs. They are dynamic managers working for the future, and are determined to take their companies into new dimensions.

Why have the Swedes been so successful?

Marcus Wallenberg, the driving force

While researching dynamic European companies I kept coming across dynamic Swedish firms. Gradually I formed the impression that, certainly as far as the larger companies are concerned, the Swedes are especially dynamic. We looked at three Swedish companies for this book, Electrolux, ASEA and IKEA, and there are plenty of other examples. Esselte has made its mark in office communications; SAS is one of the most successful European airlines; Tetrapak leads the world in drink packaging. Atlas Copco, Saab–Scania, SKF, Stora and Volvo are all successful Swedish companies.

Such above-average success is surprising, since Sweden is not well situated geographically and its only significant natural resource is iron. Besides, the economic and political situation in this extravagant socialist state is anything but favourable.

One explanation for Sweden's economic success has been put forward by Michael Porter in his study of the international competitiveness of nations. Porter's argument is that difficult conditions, far from inevitably bringing negative consequences, often force companies to perform well, especially in innovation, with the result that they have the advantage in international competition.[1] This was borne out by Hans Werthén, the President of Electrolux, in our discussion of his company's strategy of internationalization: 'Commercial openings for Electrolux in Sweden were so restricted by the socialist state that the long-term development of the company could only be assured by consistent internationalization. We had no choice: we had to look for our success abroad!'

But Swedish economic policy alone cannot totally explain the dynamism of Swedish companies. It could equally well have led to apathy and decline, as was seen in the Britain of the 1950s and 1960s, for example. Another factor would therefore appear to be much more important: the flourishing entrepreneurial climate in the higher echelons of Swedish industry. Many Swedish companies show a thirst for action and a will to expand, along with a readiness to take risks.

The driving force behind this entrepreneurial atmosphere is without doubt the industrialist Marcus Wallenberg. During the 1960s he developed a group of managers whose ultimate goal was the expansion of their companies. The powerful dynamic culture of this group spread out to people much further away. The successes of the 1970s and 1980s must have reinforced their dynamic behaviour; there was a widespread feeling that they were going somewhere. Swedish success can therefore also be attributed to Marcus Wallenberg's standards of dynamism and expansion.

The importance of the social climate

It is clear from the Swedish example that is possible to breed corporate dynamics over a wide range of companies. Common attitudes evolve within a fairly close group which lead to all the companies involved becoming dynamic. Such attitudes might include:

- We find it worthwhile to work towards growth and expansion. We think that multiplying turnover and profit quickly constitutes success.
- We want our activities to extend worldwide (so we multiply).
- We make a conscious effort to follow unconventional, direct routes.
- We are ready to take risks.
- We intend to work hard for our success.

These attitudes, widespread in Sweden in the 1970s and 1980s, are in direct contrast to the conservative approach of Switzerland, West Germany and some other countries. Here the dominant values tend to be stability and security, with rewards coming to those who make the fewest mistakes. Anyone whose success is greater than average is watched with envy; certain failure is predicted for them, and if it comes then the gloating is great.

Industry-wide patterns are enormously important. History shows that the major developments – and I should like to include the energization of the economy among these – are always supported by groups and arise in 'clusters'. This was true of the Italian Renaissance and of French impressionism; the business world has such a cluster in Silicon Valley.

Almost all great economic successes are attributed to individuals. People such as Lee Iacocca, Helmut Maucher or Akio Morita become legends in their own lifetime. Certainly many of the major organizations have been built up by gifted entrepreneurs who have had the insight and vision, and especially the energy and ability, to get things done. But is a dynamic company the exclusive work of an individual?

Interestingly enough, many of the businessmen I talked to said that dynamism was always generated by a committed team. They thought that the business press and the management staff attribute success retrospectively to one person because of the human need to keep things simple.

It is impossible to define the true entrepreneur and growth promoter. Typical cases might include the following:

- An individual who develops dynamism because of his or her inner drive.
- An individual who develops dynamism because of their relationship with the outside world (as in the Swedish example).

- All the members of a management team that evolves dynamic group values as guiding principles.

Both individuals and management groups can be promoters of dynamism. Their motives and behaviour are sometimes socially dictated.

The growth promoter's character and situation

Character and ambition

There is no typical growth promoter. Just as Kotter established that successful general managers display quite different personality traits,[2] so do growth promoters. The architect of the Finnish company Nokia, Kari Kairamo, who died not long ago, was regarded as an extremely active entrepreneur and manager, and his employees aptly dubbed him 'the turbo'. In contrast Dr Curt Nicolin, the equally successful President of ASEA, is seen as quieter and more thoughtful, though he can be very energetic in action.

However, that does not mean that no character traits and abilities are specific to entrepreneurs. There has been a line of research since the beginning of the twentieth century on the assumption of the classic personality theory that '...leadership comes from particularly prominent characteristics of the leader, which are independent of the situation, task and group'.[3] Recent research on this theme in the USA includes work by Bennis and Nanus, Boyatzis, Hornstein, Kotter, Kouzes and Posner, and Moss-Kanter. These authors have picked out the following key abilities which we can reformulate to fit growth promoters:[4]

- Growth promoters can develop and communicate visions. They concentrate on the spiritual and emotional resources of the organization.
- Growth promoters actively initiate change; they are ready to experiment and to take risks.
- Growth promoters model the development of their company. They put visions into coherent action and lead 'by doing'.
- Growth promoters have the ability to put together cohesive management teams, and actively involve their fellow managers in making and implementing decisions. 'Leaders make others feel like owners, not like hired hands.'[5]
- Growth promoters are 'social architects'. Through their ability to communicate they make a lasting impression on the culture of their company, and often implement their decisions indirectly by building

up a network of cooperative relationships around themselves.

- Growth promoters have distinct conceptual abilities which enable them to convert vague ideas and aims into coherent action.
- Growth promoters are action-oriented. Karl Weick of Cornell puts it like this: 'Chaotic action is preferable to orderly inaction.'[6]

All this must be qualified, since it relates directly to personality theory. Current management theory rightly casts doubt on the attribution of success to a few character traits, regardless of entrepreneurial situation, political conditions, luck and coincidence.[7]

My own research indicates that determination to take the company into new dimensions is often a noticeable characteristic of growth promoters. Many start out with little or no idea of the value potential which will make expansion possible for them, but their ambition is such that they set out to find it. They may make several false starts before hitting on the right potential. The story of Moritz Suter, founder of Crossair AG, illustrates this pattern. In 1976 Suter started an air taxi business, and two years later he tried an aircraft leasing company; neither of these made the breakthrough for him. His third venture was to found a regional airline, Crossair. Here at last he had found extremely attractive value potential, and he has developed it with great talent.

It is interesting, however, that several executives of dynamic companies told me that expansive growth was not their primary goal at all. Of course they were willing to take the opportunity to expand, but expansion was not seen as an aim in itself. Their companies have grown because of the demand for their products. High performance has generated its own growth. This is the prevalent view in companies such as Hanson plc, Cartier and Amexco. Like many other firms, these companies only permit growth as long as they can maintain the high yields they expect.

In this case the company is usually already turning out a product which answers a particular need: the value potential is precisely defined. At first the growth promoter scarcely thinks of expansion, but a dynamic is born anyway and sweeps him or her along. Bill Bowerman is an experienced athletics trainer who was concerned about the number of foot injuries sustained by sportsmen. He realized that sports shoes were totally inadequate for high performance and in the early 1960s he set himself to solve the problem. The shoes he designed for his athletes had lighter soles, yet supported and cushioned the foot better than their predecessors had done. They soon made a name for themselves in sporting circles. Philip Knight, a young man who had trained under Bowerman, decided to set up a marketing system for his shoes, and started a company with Bowerman as his partner. The company was renamed Nike Inc. (after the Greek winged goddess of victory) in 1971. Nike shoes, originally designed for a handful of athletes, sold like hot cakes, and Nike Inc. was forced to expand. Bowerman and Knight had had no desire at all to build up a millionaire company; in this case the dynamic growth sprang entirely from the extremely attractive value potential.

In other words, there are two different types of growth promoter, each with different levels of ambition. The first type has an urge to expand and wants to create something big for the sake of it. The second type is not so obsessed with success, but develops a particular product or service which turns out to be the key to very attractive value potential, and brings success.

Power to act

The growth promoter's position in the hierarchy and the degree of autonomy which it bestows determine how much he or she is able to do. A sole shareholder who is both president of the company and managing director can introduce as many dynamic measures as she likes, while in a public company the interests of the voting shareholders must always be taken into account. A chairman of the board may find he has to persuade both the board and top management to go his way. Where management is responsible for the day-to-day operations of the company the chairman cannot disregard the normal channels.

Growth promoters in middle management are even more restricted, especially if they work for a static company. Their influence is so limited that they have only one course of action open to them: I shall come to that later.

Value potential

Finally, the company's position in relation to value potential has a strong influence on the entrepreneur's activities.

Has the company already found a concept which will allow dynamic expansion? Ray Kroc found himself in this happy position, when in 1955 he took over the concept of fast food restaurants which had been developed by the McDonald brothers and started to expand it through franchises. The market potential and the concept which would tap it (McDonald's restaurants, and the franchise concept) were already in existence. Kroc's great achievement lay in multiplying the restaurants very quickly, following a deliberate policy of expansion.

In many cases, however, there seems to be hardly any value potential, say, in a turnaround situation. At the end of the 1970s SAS, which was very bureaucratic at that time, was generating hardly any profits at all. Its new head, Jan Carlzon, had to find new value potential and develop a new product concept to fit it. He focused on the market potential in the business travel sector and came up with a new service for it, business class. He conceived an integrated system of services from hotel check-ins to business lounges.[8] With this new concept in place the company was able to expand again. Turnover climbed from 10,000m. SKr in 1981 to 22,000m. SKr in 1986. In 1981 there had been losses on paper of 51m. SKr, but in 1986 the company showed a profit of 1,500m. SKr.

Often the owner–manager faces the problem of unsatisfactory value potential, and his first plan to improve the situation ends in failure. Fritz Maurer, successful entrepreneur and now the only tyre producer in Switzerland, started out roasting coffee, but in the 1930s this became ever more difficult as the potential began to fade away. Being a bold entrepreneur, Maurer changed track to the production of tyres, realizing, in the run-up to the Second World War, that there would be interesting value potential in the supply of parts for armaments. When the war came he was in a position to tap this potential.

A situation where there is no value potential worth mentioning clearly calls for a different management approach to the company which is exploiting great potential. The presence or absence of value potential has an important influence on what the growth promoter can do.

Styles of behaviour

We have seen that the behaviour of growth promoters will be influenced by their own personality and ambitions, their place in the hierarchy and the freedom they have to act, as well as the state of the company's value potential. Taking all these into consideration, the entrepreneurial growth promoter can follow one or more of five typical styles:

1   Coaching
2   Pushing
3   Accelerating
4   Exploiting
5   Infiltrating

Style 1: Coaching

In the 1970s, the markets served by ASEA AB had largely lost their attraction. Relatively stagnant turnover and, in particular, a sharp drop in profits indicated that the value potential of the company's activities was disappearing. Dr Curt Nicolin was President of the Board of ASEA, as well as a number of other companies, including SAS. He was one of Marcus

Wallenberg's disciples and had correspondingly high ambitions for business development.

However, even with his strong position in the hierarchy, Nicolin could exert only a limited influence. He had neither the time nor the detailed knowledge to do anything on the operational level, and in any case Swedish law stipulates that operational management is not a function of the president of the board, drawing a sharp distinction between that office and the rest of the board members.

In this situation, Nicolin had to resort to a style of indirect action. Firstly he had to appoint a chief executive who could initiate and maintain operational dynamism. In 1980 Nicolin found the right person in the shape of Percy Barnevik, and their subsequent cooperation was to prove extremely fruitful. Nicolin created the freedom necessary for dynamic development and sheltered Barnevik from undesirable interference and criticism. He also made a point of motivating the operational managers.

This is how coaching works:

1   Corporate dynamism stands or falls with the operational manager, so it is most important to find the right person for this job. Curt Nicolin's achievement lay in finding Percy Barnevik and signing him on. For the sake of completeness we should mention that he was just as successful with his other companies, appointing Carlzon to SAS, for example, and Eskilsson to ESAB, the world leader in welding machines.

2   One of the main tasks in coaching is to protect the operational management from disturbance. The ever-present critics and doubters must be held back, so that the operational head can apply himself wholeheartedly to dynamic development.

3   It is important to ensure the motivation of the operational head and his management through personal contact. This task must not be underestimated. There are always setbacks to be coped with, and the coach must provide the necessary moral support. The right atmosphere of motivation can also be created by rewarding the success of operational management with performance-based incentives.

In the example we have used there was no discernible value potential. Coaching can also be appropriate, and even easier, where attractive value potential is readily available. It is not surprising, then, that coaching is a common style of dynamic leadership.

The role of the coach is often appropriate to an older manager handing over to the younger generation, especially perhaps in family firms. Many entrepreneurs have put great energy into the dynamic development of the company over the years, but there comes a point where they have to restrict themselves to the role of coach, which can require enormous self-control.

This exercise was skilfully mastered by Professor Martin Hilti, the head of the Hilti Group. He handed over control to his son Michael and the rest of the board at the right time, and created the necessary space for the company's future management. From then on he guided the fate of the company as a whole from an elevated observation point. The excellent results recently achieved by the Hilti Group prove him right. Growth figures are high and profits above average. No less important, the management team is a very strong one.

Style 2: Pushing

The situation for entrepreneurial chief executives or managing directors is quite different. Their hierarchical position gives them freedom of action and a direct influence on the operations of the company. Where there is very little value potential in evidence, the style of dynamic management used will be pushing.

In the mid-1970s Kari Kairamo became head of Nokia, a Finnish conglomerate specializing in traditional activities such as cable, tyre and paper manufacture. Its turnover was just under 2,000m. Finnmarks in 1975. Kairamo's ambitions could not be satisfied by optimizing these mature activities: he wanted to venture into new dimensions. Nokia had a very limited involvement in the manufacture of radio equipment, and here Kairamo saw synergies which could be exploited as the basis of a dynamic expansion in the electronic sector. In less than twelve years Nokia's turnover increased more than tenfold, to 21,500m. Finnmarks.

Kairamo expanded principally by acquiring electronics firms. Some were in growth markets, but others, such as the television companies Salora in Finland, Luxor in Sweden and Oceanic in France, were more sluggish, because the value potential in their markets was only modest. Kairamo had to exert his personal influence intensively to ensure dynamic development.

The main methods of pushing are:

- *Employing new management.* Kairamo employed new, sometimes very young, 'hungry' managers to many of the most challenging management positions. With this new blood the hardest tasks were tackled quickly and easily, with great creativity. Above all these fresh managers were not bound by obsolete historical constraints.
- *Intensive personal influence.* Markus Wallenberg, for example, telephoned his key personnel at any time of the day or night, and at the weekend.
- *Setting ambitious goals.* Kari Kairamo was able to achieve his

demanding goals for reorganization and profits by strong personal contact and by constantly checking on progress.

As we have said, pushing is principally used where attractive value potential is slight or where it is difficult to exploit it. The object of generating dynamism in such a case is to make the most of an existing business activity or to make new value potential fruitful by ensuring a high level of commitment. Even organizations at a standstill can often be energized from above by the growth promoter's influence.

Style 3: Accelerating

There was plenty of attractive value potential for Hans Werthén of Electrolux in 1967. Many small white goods manufacturers had problems, and lacked the will and often the resources to change their structures so that they could survive in the sector. They were ripe for takeover, and Electrolux was in a position to exploit this tremendous value potential. It had the necessary management potential for reorganization, as well as the requisite production and marketing know-how. It also had access to potential finance – even if only a limited amount. There was so much value potential that the takeovers became easier as more were made: the more firms Electrolux acquired the more people knew of its policy of takeovers and the more companies offered themselves for sale. Hans Werthén was in a wholly different situation to Kari Kairamo, and did not have to rely on his personal influence to generate the dynamics. His task was to establish a rhythm for the takeovers.

Werthén was very ambitious and was determined to expand fast. His strong hierarchical position as managing director and later president enabled him to encourage dynamic development through his own influence. He was in an ideal position to multiply the benefits for all stakeholders, which he succeeded in doing on a very wide basis throughout the 22 years of his involvement.

The heads of some of the other companies in my survey found themselves in a similar position. Moritz Suter of Crossair, who discovered the value potential for a regional airline in Europe in 1978, has been able to open no fewer than 20 routes since 1979. Ingvar Kamprad's IKEA furniture shops generated much higher value than other distribution systems at the time, and this high value potential has enabled him to open over 70 new furniture shops in the last fifteen years.

In all these cases the heads of the firms recognized great value potential which was being insufficiently developed, and, because of their ambition, determined to make the most of it. Timing is extremely important in such a case. The value potential needs to be developed as fast as possible in order to reach the all-important strategic excellence position before the competition does. The growth promoter must therefore concentrate on accelerating the whole process of developing the value potential.

In the accelerating style the entrepreneur saves his own time by working by exception. When everything is going well he gives a free rein, but when problems arise he intervenes. Problems are likely to be few, however, because the value potential is clearly defined and easily recognizable. The world welcomes the company's output, which makes everything much easier.

Naturally acceleration also means setting ambitious goals and carrying them through. Every available incentive is employed in the deliberate drive to expand. Employee participation in turnover and profits helps to involve key managers both materially and psychologically in the growth of the company.

Style 4: Exploiting

The fourth style of dynamic management is typical of those who have tapped into substantial value potential but have no personal urge to expand.

Jerry Kohlberg developed the financial innovation of the leveraged buyout (LBO) to develop some of the most interesting value potential of the late twentieth century. Within a very short time Kohlberg and his partners in Kohlberg, Kravis, Roberts (KKR) were being offered financial resources by the thousand million. It was never Kohlberg's intention to expand. The company grew because of the momentum created by the enormous value potential: investors quickly recognized that LBO funds were very profitable and eagerly placed enormous financial resources with them. This enabled Kohlberg to look for new takeover targets and make new buyouts. It is typical of Kohlberg that he actually left KKR, which he had founded, because he was unwilling to expand as much as his partners, Kravis and Roberts, wanted to.

There are certainly situations like this, where unsuspected value potential is stumbled upon, and the growth promoter can simply exploit the possibilities as far as he feels is justified. Exploiting is a rather passive style compared with acceleration. Expansion may even be deliberately stifled, as in the case of Cartier, which is now very selective in the new jewellery shops it opens.

The exploiting growth promoter simply lets the expansionist forces take effect, and ensures that expansion does not overstretch the company. The management style is characterized by delegation, with the growth promoter watching over the key financial data and setting the general direction of the company.

Style 5: Infiltrating

Any manager can be a growth promoter, not just top management. In very bureaucratic companies it often happens that higher management puts on the brakes, while some (often younger) managers are ambitious for the organization and want it to expand. They may have spotted interesting value potential which top management has overlooked.

Dynamic development is more difficult in such a situation, but there is no reason to give it up. The dynamic process can be set in motion by skilful manœuvring.

The managing director of the German subsidiary of an American company was only concerned to maintain the company's existing position. As a result the company was actually losing market share, and turnover was stagnating. The marketing director, the technical director and the personnel director, all younger men, were unhappy with this frustrating situation. They wanted to take the considerable opportunities offered in the marketplace by expanding. Unfortunately the managing director was in a very strong position because of his history as a financial whizzkid –in the USA they still thought of him as 'Mr Profit' – and so getting rid of him was out of the question. The three young managers developed an alternative strategy: the personnel director, who was on excellent terms with the company president in the USA, undertook to 'praise the managing director away to the United States'. He proceeded to point out the md's supposed achievements at every opportunity. It worked. A year later the managing director was promoted to the head office in the USA. The former marketing director was put in charge of the German branch, and very soon he and his team had put in hand a multitude of measures which led to great dynamic growth. Market share, turnover and profit all started to develop in a very pleasing way. Their unconventional strategy had enabled the three growth promoters to create the right political conditions for dynamic development.

There is a surprising punchline, however. After two years the president in the USA noticed that the ex-managing director simply was not fulfilling their expectations, and sent him straight back to Germany. Thereupon the three younger growth promoters resigned, and all three now occupy top positions in other companies.

What are the characteristics of the infiltration style?

The first objective is to remove the tendency of top management to preserve the status quo. To do this the growth promoter enters into coalitions with other like-minded people on the board, or in executive or middle management. The Swedish example has shown us that support groups can even be formed across the top management of different companies. The aim is to build up as large a group as possible to confront the management with dynamic ideas and gradually wear them down.

Secondly, actions speak louder than words. Growth promoters will set an example by introducing and carrying out successful dynamic projects within their own sphere of responsibility.

Of course, in practice growth promoters will not slavishly follow the scheme of action that I have described. They must develop their own style to suit the particular circumstances and their own preferences and skills. The position in relation to value potential, and the growth promoter's sphere of influence, are important factors.

It is crucial to bear in mind that value potential, and influence, will change in the course of time. The style may need to be adapted accordingly. It can of course be difficult to change from one style, or combination of styles, to another, but the successful growth promoter will cope with the problems and be able to suit the style to the prevailing situation.

Figure 4.1 illustrates the different dynamic styles.

The political process

Growth promoters always find themselves confronted in practice with the problem of how to carry their ideas through. It is quite exceptional to find the entire management of a company agreeing that corporate dynamism is both desirable and necessary. Usually there is a Gaussian distribution, with a few champions of dynamic growth at one end, a few vehement opponents of expansion at the other, and a large undecided group in the middle. As we have seen, the economic position of the company plays an important role in shaping opinion. The worse things look for the company, the more readily will management recognize the necessity of becoming dynamic.

Some growth promoters will find it impossible to wait until the pressure caused by poor results becomes unbearable. Once they have seen the need for dynamism they will be keen to make the necessary changes before the situation grows worse. In this case the political process becomes crucial. The aim is to sway the right managers, and enough of them, in favour of corporate dynamism. A political analysis should be carried out before any action can be taken:

- How powerful is the position of the growth promoter(s)?
- What is the company's situation and how does it affect the management's attitude to dynamics?
- Which managers are by nature in favour of dynamics, and which against?

Situation/measures	Dynamic style				
	Coaching	Pushing	Accelerating	Exploiting	Infiltrating
Situation					
Level of ambition	high	high	high	less significant	high
Hierarchical position	no direct operational influence	direct influence	direct influence	direct influence	subordinate position
Attraction of value potential	variable	low	high	high	recognizable
Dynamic measures	appointment of new managers	setting direct goals	motivation/incentives	delegation	enter into coalitions
	motivation	intensive influence	direct influence	skilful guidance	example (show how it works)
	protection	strict checks on success		allow external demand to take effect	

Figure 4.1 *Overview of styles of dynamic management*

- How do other stakeholders, such as shareholders, non-executive directors, unions, customers, etc., feel about dynamic growth? Could any of them be allies?

If there are clear answers to these questions then the growth promoter will be able to work out and implement a strategy. Let's take some examples.

Kari Kairamo was a very strong-willed growth promoter and was known as a pusher. As president of Nokia he had complete authority, but the company was over a hundred years old, and he had to overcome the resistance of various managers. As discussed earlier, one way he did this was by appointing young, 'hungry' managers, even to top management positions. Of the ten-strong central executive in 1988 four members were under forty and another four were less than fifty.

The president of another industrial concern was in favour of dynamic development but felt too old to take on the burdens and risks involved. Besides, some of his older colleagues were reluctant about, if not downright opposed to, going in this direction. Profits were down, and some action was vital, so the president asked an extremely able member of the executive to come up with a project to improve profits. Thus the director grew into the role of growth promoter. Together with some allies within the company he developed a group of measures to harness new value potential. At the same time he made sure he had the support of the positively-minded members of the board, and was careful to keep the 'neutral' directors well informed and motivated. With much diplomacy he even succeeded in dispelling the opposition of his negatively-minded colleagues. He had gradually created a breeding-ground for dynamic growth.

Of course the situation can be reversed. Two active members of the board of a medium-sized service company felt that the company should be expanding dynamically to take advantage of the opportunities in the business environment. The chairman of the board, however, had private ambitions outside the company and so had no desire to take on the burdens of dynamic growth. He began a game of intrigue with some loyal employees, playing off the two growth promoters against each other – which was easy enough as both only worked part-time for the company. In the end the growth promoters resigned. The company did perform quite well in the boom of the mid-1980s, but the chance to become market leader was irrevocably lost.

Corporate dynamism is very hard to define, and the growth promoter must handle the political process with the utmost creativity. At the same time he must be careful to set realistic goals and not to overstep the limits. Before trying to initiate a dynamic he should assess the situation from two angles:

The growth promoter's own position in the hierarchy and sphere of influence can be strong, eg when the promoter has a lot of power as president or managing director, or may be weak, if the promoter is a middle manager in a sluggish company.

The situation of the company is favourable if the company is already under pressure or if there are irresistibly obvious opportunities. It is unfavourable when the value potential is heading towards maturity and the company's results are still good.

Situation

		Favourable	*Unfavourable*
Position/ personal influence	*Strong*	directly implement change	create pressure
	Weak	forge coalitions	leave

Figure 4.2 *The different political tactics of the growth promoter*

From these criteria we can derive a matrix (Figure 4.2) to show the four typical courses of action:

- If the growth promoter has a strong position and the situation is favourable, then the dynamic process can be quickly and easily introduced.
- If the promoter's position is strong but the situation is unfavourable – perhaps profit levels are still satisfactory, then the promoter needs to create artificial pressure.
- If the promoter's position is weak but the company's situation is favourable, then he or she can forge coalitions. She will use creative means to try to influence the power groups in such a way that the dynamic can finally be triggered off.
- If the promoter is in a weak position and the situation is unfavourable for dynamic development, then I recommend that the promoter find a new job as quickly as possible; the company is sure to become more and more bureaucratic and will be less fun to work in the longer it goes on.

It is important to create the right balance of power in the company, otherwise it is impossible to instigate and sustain the dynamic.

Guidelines for management

Who are growth promoters?

In our sense a growth promoter is anyone who actively encourages the dynamic development of the company. The term covers owner–managers, chairmen of the board, managing directors, executive and non-executive directors, as well as entrepreneurial managers at the middle and lower levels.

The importance of the growth promoter

Growth promoters initiate the corporate dynamic and, because of their character and the way they behave, lead the company on to new horizons.

Inner drive

Entrepreneurial people are not content to be mediocre: they set themselves ambitious goals. Dynamic companies, too, set themselves high standards in order to expand.

The political process

The entrepreneurial manager uses the appropriate tactics to ensure that the political conditions within the company will allow for dynamic development.

Entrepreneurial behaviour

Five different styles of dynamic management, or a combination of them, can be used according to the circumstances. The deciding factors include the growth promoter's personal ambitions, their position in the hierarchy, and the company's situation as far as value potential is concerned.

Notes

1   See Porter, 1988.
2   See Kotter, 1982, pp. 34ff.
3   See Wunderer and Grunwald, 1980, p. 113.
4   See Bennis and Nanus, 1985; Boyatzis, 1982; Hornstein, 1986; Kotter, 1982 and 1985; Kouzes and Posner, 1988; Moss-Kanter, 1983.
5   Kouzes and Posner, 1988, p. 131.

6   Quoted in Peters and Waterman, 1982, p. 134.
7   Cf. the exhaustive review of this line of research in Wunderer and Grunwald, 1980, pp. 122 ff.
8   Carlzon, 1987, pp. 39-51.

Part II

Corporate dynamism in practice

The first four chapters of the book have described the principles of corporate dynamism, the foundations for the management of the dynamic company. Now we come to the application of those principles, especially in five key areas:

- The corporate concept or corporate strategy
- Organizational structures
- Man-management
- The time factor
- Minimizing the risks involved.

I could of course have looked at other aspects, such as the relationship between planning or management systems and corporate dynamism, but in our analysis of dynamic companies these five points seemed dominant, so I have chosen to concentrate on them.

Chapter 5

The corporate concept: a practical guideline

The dynamic principle hinges on value potential. The growth promoter needs firstly to establish the state of the value potential which is relevant to his or her company. On the basis of this a corporate concept can be developed which will assist corporate dynamism. Let us look at both stages.

New questions for the dynamic manager

In classic management theory the development of a corporate concept or strategy is preceded by a number of analyses, including the standard analyses of the business environment, the industry, the market, the competition, and the company's own strengths and weaknesses, as well as specific strategic analyses of the value chains[1] or fields of activity.[2]

The managers of a dynamic company, however, will be more interested in certain other aspects relevant to its future development. The growth promoter needs to bear four questions in mind:

- What benefits should the company be creating for its stakeholders?
- How far advanced is the value potential exploited by the company, and how does this affect the company's strategy?
- What value potential could the company start to develop in the future?

- How can business activities be multiplied?

Who should benefit from the company?

The ultimate aim of every company is to generate benefits for its stakeholders. In Chapter 1 the major stakeholders of the company are named as:

- Customers
- Workforce
- (Upper) management[3]
- Investors (shareholders)
- Suppliers
- The community at large (borough, region, nation, etc.)

This list can be enlarged at will.

Any discussion of corporate dynamism must start by asking to what extent and in what broad areas benefits should be generated. In other words, what level is the company aiming at? Does dynamic expansion seem to be desirable, or is the company justifiably complacent and in no need of dynamic development? If dynamics are to be generated, is the idea to achieve a substantial increase in benefits by every means available, or should there be a limited and precisely defined objective? The question of risk also arises, since strong expansion obviously entails greater risks.[4]

Having established the general level of expectations, ie the basic expansion policy, you will need to work out what priority to give the various interest groups. Should the customers be most important, as is more or less the case with Migro, the large Swiss retailer? Is the company there to provide secure jobs for its workers, and satisfy the unions? Or should it focus primarily on shareholder value, as do many companies in the USA?[5]

For dynamic management to succeed the desired extent of expansion and the priority of the different interest groups must be clear and unequivocal. It would, however, be unrealistic to make corporate dynamism dependent on these two questions alone. In practice the distribution of power among the individual interest groups rarely reflects their various claims to power, making for a complex situation in the majority of companies. As a result many of the people involved in deciding the allocation of priorities are unwilling to put all their cards on the table.

Good managers are aware of these problems and try to reach a consensus which is acceptable to all parties. Such a consensus is perhaps one of the most distinctive characteristics of the companies we looked at.

What phase has the value potential reached?

We saw in Chapter 2 that value potential tends to go through certain phases, with different levels of attraction. It is essential to know how far the value potential exploited by your company has developed, since this will have a critical effect on corporate dynamism. Careful consideration should be given to the questions displayed in Figure 5.1.

- Is the value potential still emerging?
- If the value potential has reached the growth phase, is it at the beginning, or has it already progressed quite far?
- Has it entered the mature phase or even slipped into decline?
- How will the potential develop in the future?
- If the company is simultaneously exploiting several different kinds of value potential, have they reached different phases?

Figure 5.1 *Basic questions derived from the phase model*

It is not easy to answer these questions in practice. Forecasts are always a matter of opinion. However, some valid, objective information can be obtained. It is often worth looking at the past development of the value potential, for example:

- It is relatively easy to assess market potential in many established consumer and investment firms. Here there are usually valid data to be had on the number of actual and potential customers, the volume of consumption, the level of saturation and so on. With careful analysis it is generally possible to judge fairly precisely the development phase of the value potential. For instance, it is obvious that, in an age of growing awareness of health, the markets for tobacco, spirits and chocolate are becoming saturated or declining. Just as obviously, the market for compact discs is still growing.
- Equally there are no particular problems for companies such as Electrolux, which exploit the value potential of acquisitions within a certain sector. Here it is easy to find out the number of targets still available for acquisition. With Hanson plc there is more scope for argument. On the one hand 'undermanaged companies', with a significantly lower book value than real value, are becoming harder to find because of the swelling wave of restructuring; on the other hand it can be argued that any economy will always contain some poorly managed companies.
- At the other extreme, it is most difficult to estimate the value potential of highly innovative products in the emergent phase. In this

case the development of the potential can seldom be ascertained in advance.

Generally speaking the greatest problem lies in subjective attitudes: often top management is simply not prepared to admit that the value potential is maturing or even declining. A dynamic strategy is rejected in favour of the comfortable option of protecting assets and avoiding risks. Hence it is of the utmost importance that the analysis of all the relevant value potential is soundly based and well supported.

The analysis should make it possible to deduce whether there are still sufficient openings for the prospective development of the company or whether stagnation or decline are to be expected. For dynamic companies the latter will inevitably mean embarking on a search for new value potential. On the other hand companies in the emerging or growth phase can concentrate all the harder on exploiting their current value potential.

Each phase of development requires a different angle of analysis. Let us look briefly at the key questions in each phase.

Basic questions in the emergent phase

Is the targeted value potential sufficiently fertile?

It is often hard to tell whether sufficient business volume will result to justify putting great efforts into exploiting particular value potential. Ideas which are especially innovative are often almost impossible to judge objectively. Experts are usually critical by nature and tend to rule out potential when the possible applications are unclear, in the early stages. It is well known that in the early 1950s the experts assumed that the potential world market for electronic calculators was very small. They simply could not imagine the present situation. The same is true for all other emerging value potential.

In these circumstances it is extremely difficult to form a proper picture of the value potential. Lateral thinking is the secret of good judgement in this case, and experience is of no value at all. Quite the reverse: preconceptions can lead to the fertility of the value potential simply being dismissed. That is why many established companies fail to exploit new opportunities and why many branches of industry are revolutionized by outsiders. Theodore Levitt dealt with this subject in his famous article 'Marketing Myopia'.[6] He demonstrated, for example, that the newly emerging value potential of air transport was not developed by established transport companies (rail and road) but by newly set up outsider companies. Nor did established companies achieve the breakthrough of the innovative electronic clock. I was witness to an analogous case in my practice when the major computer manufacturers laughed at the minicomputers and new data processing concepts produced by Digital Equipment and Hewlett-Packard. They continued to concentrate on large mainframe computers, thus leaving the field clear for Digital Equipment to open up the market for minicomputers. Digital was to become the second largest computer manufacturer in the world.

This is a clear example of the difficulty of assessing the productivity of emerging potential. The large manufacturers were unanimous for quite a long time that minicomputers were a speciality with insignificant market potential. Olson of Digital, and Hewlett and Packard, on the other hand, gambled successfully on the new value potential.

How should the value potential be developed?

This question brings us to the setting up of processes and systems. Ways have to be found to exploit the value potential. In the classic case the aim is to conceive a new product designed for an identifiable potential market. But interesting value potential is to be found in all possible areas, both external and internal, so more unconventional ideas should be tested, far beyond mere product categories. Often much greater potential can be developed by process or system innovation.

Where the value potential is in the emergent phase, the central task is to build up business activities directed towards it. The new concept must be noticeably different from its predecessor from the point of view of the relevant stakeholders, and clearly provide greater value. In the case of product innovation the higher value might mean that the product is, say, more functional or easier to use, or has a more pleasing design.

With new processes the emphasis is often on efficiency and cost-cutting. But speed of production is becoming ever more important. Process innovations are also used to improve effectiveness. 3M, for instance, has worked for a long time on its innovation process in order to reach its present high standards of product development and introduction.

The objectives are similar with systems. The Metro wholesale store costs much less to run than competing methods of distribution, so the new system led to increased cost-efficiency. The benefits of some other systems are more qualitative: the atmosphere of a Cartier bijouterie offers a special buying experience. Innovative systems may work much faster. Benetton, as is well known, developed an integrated computer system linking shops to warehouses and production units, thus substantially shortening the procurement cycle.

Setting up processes and systems in the emergent phase is very demanding. The ground rules are treated in detail in other publications and so are only briefly touched on here:[7]

- There should be close relations with everyone affected. The success of a new product depends on it being developed in close cooperation with the customers, and the same principle applies to all processes which exploit value potential. Thus, for example, the purchasing process must be set up in collaboration with the relevant suppliers.

• Constant testing is vital. In new territory there is bound to be uncertainty as to which innovation efforts will win through in the end. For this reason innovative companies move faster than their competitors from the drawing board to lifelike tests.[8] The whole concept can be tested, as well as the individual parts. In the first case, for instance, different variations of a new product will be tried out. In the second case, perhaps the layouts for the new system (eg a Benetton shop) are tested for customer acceptability.

The basic questions in the emergent phase are summarized in Figure 5.2.

• Is the value potential under consideration sufficiently fertile?
• Is our judgement of the value potential sufficiently objective or are we still thinking in outdated ways?
• How well do the company's products fit the requirements of the value potential?
• How can the value potential be developed?
• What benefit is to be generated?
• What processes could be multiplied?
• To what extent could the value potential be exploited by system multiplication?
• How could the new concepts be tested?

Figure 5.2 *Basic questions in the emergent phase*

Basic questions in the growth phase

Value potential expands in the growth phase, but the nature of this expansion can vary tremendously. In one case it is short but intensive, with a lasting effect, in another more moderate and sustained or even cyclic. The important point is how long the growth will last.

Multiplication is the central task in the growth phase. In order to multiply successfully you need to think which other firms or organizations will be adversely affected by your expansion, and anticipate their reactions as carefully as in a game of chess. Suitable countermeasures have to be planned.

Promising value potential will soon attract other companies which have recognized the commercial value and want to develop it for themselves.

For example, it took only about three years for the co-marketing idea to be adapted by Glaxo's competitors. So in the growth phase you must watch carefully to see if other companies join the pursuit of the growing value potential.

In the early growth phase multiplication can usually be quite systematic, but as growth progresses activities will need to be modified in line with the changing situation.

Expansion in the growth phase must not overstretch your resources, and a watchful eye should be kept to ensure that the limits are not overstepped.

The basic questions for the growth phase are presented in Figure 5.3.

- What is the extent of the available value potential?
- What are the probable influences, good or bad, of the business environment on the future development of the potential?
- What are the likely reactions, if any, of new or existing competitors?
- Is there new value potential emerging which would complement the existing potential if the two were developed together?
- How much modification is necessary and what should it be?
- Which particular skills (strategic excellence positions) must the company develop and build up so that the value potential can be successfully exploited?
- What standard concept could be adequately multiplied?
- Is technical or process standardization possible?
- What operational problems are likely to be faced in multiplication?
- What measures could be taken to avoid the problems or reduce them in advance? How could risks be cut down?

Figure 5.3 *Basic questions in the growth phase*

Basic questions in the mature phase

Managers are often so set in their ways that they fail to recognize when value potential is maturing. This happened to many Swiss clock makers in the 1970s. The head of a famous clock factory told me in 1974 that electronic watches would never retail for less than 500 SFr. because the costs were too high. His prophecy was supported by a technological market survey carried out by a very well-known research institute. How could a forecast be so wrong? The reason is mind set. Many clock factories were steeped in tradition. Their managers had often studied clock making at special schools, and spent their entire careers making mechanical clocks. All their personal contacts had followed the same path. To these people it was quite unthinkable that mechanical clocks could be replaced by electronic ones. They simply had not noticed that Swiss retailers were selling electronic clocks for less than 300 SFr. in 1974!

This situation is typical: the people in the politically important positions do not notice that the market is nearly glutted. Their successes in the growth phase have boosted their self-confidence and self-esteem. They are convinced that the saturation is temporary, blaming it for instance on the prevailing economic climate. They are too confident to see sense, and think that the essential corrective measures are unnecessary. This is a basic problem in overcoming maturity.

In such situations management must be alerted to the dangers of mind set. The clearest possible evidence must be shown that maturity has been reached. In some cases political influence is imperative.

Maturity is recognizable because the value potential harnessed by the company begins to yield less. This diminishing fertility can be attributed to market saturation. With much value potential, however, there are simply not enough targets left. This is particularly true of internal value potential, whose volume is generally limited from the start. For example, balance sheet potential is exhausted when all assets and liabilities have been deployed to best effect. It also holds, though, for takeover strategies in industries which are already fairly concentrated.

Often at this stage there is increasing pressure on margins. The usual reaction in such situations is to tighten up management. Cost-cutting programmes are instigated and stricter controls are introduced. These activities are on the whole a good thing, but problems arise when tightening up leads to increased bureacracy. Managers retreat defensively behind bureaucratic regulation. The focus switches from dynamic expansion to protection. Regimentation seems to become the norm: documents such as organizational diagrams and job descriptions define precisely how everyone is to do their job, how far their authority extends, what they have to report and to whom, and so on. These allow events to be closely supervised and apparently kept on the rails. Such regimentation runs fundamentally counter to the changing business world.

The mature phase becomes critical when the company can only think and behave defensively. It loses every creative innovative tactic. It perishes in the vicious circle of inertia: because no more openings for expansion can be seen, there must be more regulation. The increasing regulation hampers such creative and innovative forces as still exist. Progressive managers leave, and only nervous bureaucrats and stick-in-the-muds apply for vacancies. So the ability to revive the company, by harnessing new value potential, is completely lost.

In many companies which show these signs the problem is most of all that their defence strategies are successful for quite a long time. They are still making a profit, even if an increasingly marginal one. Besides, they often have considerable reserves which allow them to keep their heads above water.

Instead of being defensive, though, a company with mature value potential should be looking to the future. There may be ways to exploit the existing value potential better. Skilful marketing measures can extend the life cycle of a product in the market, or it may be possible to move into other financial markets. Since, however, corporate dynamism depends on value potential with promise, companies whose potential is coming to maturity should be asking: Where can we find attractive new value potential?

In classic competitive strategy theory the search focuses on potential in the marketplace. The best known model comes from Ansoff, who distinguishes four broad possibilities:[9]

- Market penetration
- Developing a market
- Developing a product
- Diversification.

By these means it should be possible to uncover interesting new potential in new or existing markets. The problem is that as more markets are reaching saturation it is ever more difficult to find attractive market potential. That is why the dynamic approach I have developed calls for all the available external and internal value potential to be considered, not just market potential. This flexible concept is better suited than traditional competitive strategy to the turbulent world of the departing twentieth and dawning twenty-first centuries.

The survey of value potential in Chapter 2 is a good starting point for checking all external and internal value potential. In every case you should assess whether your firm could exploit it and if so how much. This will raise certain problems:

- You need to establish how much future growth can be expected. Once again prognosis, with all its objective and subjective uncertainties, is a problem, but again past experience can provide reliable information.
- New markets are very hard to assess. Generally the only aid is to test the new products in the market.
- Technological potential should normally also be subjected to concrete test programmes.
- By contrast, value potential arising from new economic conditions can be easily ascertained. This applies, for instance, to potential in liquid capital markets and especially to value potential springing from a discrepancy (usually brought about by inflation) between the company's book value and its market value. Often inexpensive

investigations can lead to unexpected openings, as long as they are unconventional and open-minded.

- In many countries there is clearly recognizable human potential. Too many firms have closed their eyes to the potential of the widespread desire for self-development and entrepreneurial activity.
- The potential implications of new legal regulations are usually identified at an early stage, and it is easy to obtain information about them.
- It is even simpler to assess internal value potential since the necessary data are available in abundance. Cost-cutting potential, organizational potential, expertise potential and especially the opportunities of asset redeployment are easy to record and analyse.

The questions for a company in the mature phase are summarized in Figure 5.4.

- How far has the process of bureaucratization advanced?
- How can the existing value potential be more extensively exploited?
- What new value potential could the company consider?
- How great is it?
- What new ideas can the company offer to harness the value potential?
- What are the opportunities and dangers of this value potential?
    - general trends in ecology, technology, economy, politics, as well as social and demographic developments
    - developments in the relevant interest groups (customers, suppliers, staff, etc.)
    - developments with competitors, who are also looking at the value potential (old and new competitors, barriers to entry, etc.)
- What strengths can the company build on in relation to the value potential? What weaknesses have to be overcome?
- Which particular abilities in the sense of strategic excellence positions must the company develop and build up so that the new value potential can be successfully harnessed?

Figure 5.4 *Basic questions in the mature phase*

All decision makers find it even more difficult to recognize attractive value potential quickly because of the almost unmanageable daily deluge of information. Besides the company's internal information, the mass media and the economic and trade press constantly deliver new information about possible new value potential, ranging from perestroika in the USSR to superconductivity and new developments in the world of finance. The problem is made greater by the Europeanization and globalization of the markets. From this flood of information which overwhelms us, often in different languages, the company must distil all the implications for existing and newly relevant value potential.

Many managers simply cut themselves off from this flood of information and fail to notice events abroad published in the economic press. This presents a great opportunity for dynamic entrepreneurs. For example: in the early 1980s Hans-Dieter Fuchs, then barely thirty years old, came across the first news of leveraged buyouts in the American economic press. He quickly recognized the value potential inherent in this new form of acquisition, and proceeded to tailor the concept of leveraged buyouts to conditions in West Germany, thus becoming a true economic pioneer. By transferring the LBO concept developed in the USA to the Federal Republic he was able to build up a group of companies with a turnover of over 400m. DM in the space of a few years.

It is absolutely essential to tap all possible sources of information in a wide-ranging, unblinkered search for value potential. Specialist firms can provide important support services here.

Basic questions in the decline phase

In the decline phase value potential shrinks. The number of possible transactions diminishes. Since costs cannot be cut in line with the reduction in transactions (because of fixed overheads for example) the company is mostly headed for an unfavourable profit situation.

The classic reactions to this situation might include (more) cost-cutting programmes or divestments. Some firms lobby for state subventions or tax concessions. Often attempts are made to bring in trade barriers or import restrictions (eg protective taxes on agricultural imports or the French restrictions on the import of cars). The value of such steps is doubtful. Far from helping to ease the situation, they actually contribute to the atrophy of the company or the sector. The experience of the European agricultural policy bears this out. Other solutions must be found.

It may seem especially desirable for declining companies to tap into new value potential with great future promise. Argenti has shown that firms in decline often take refuge in a major project. In 1967 the ailing Rolls Royce Aero Engines embarked on the RB 211 turbine project, a large-scale project which it expected to account for about a third of total turnover for the next few years. But time schedule and cost projections were both unduly optimistic, and the budget was exceeded five times over. The resulting cash crisis forced Rolls Royce to declare bankruptcy in February 1971.[10] Financial risks often rule out the development of new value potential at this late stage.

I would recommend that companies in decline should start by introducing classic turnaround management. It is often better to bring about a reasonable recovery by exploiting internal potential in this way rather than giving priority to the development of new external value potential. Helpful advice on turnaround tactics can be found in a number of other publications.[11]

Figure 5.5 summarizes the basic questions which arise in the decline phase.

- How can costs be cut and cashflow increased?
- Could turnaround management be instituted?
- What internal value potential can be developed in the short term?
- Is there new external value potential which can be developed without great risks?

Figure 5.5 *Basic questions in the decline phase*

Which value drivers increase value?

Dynamic expansion always puts a strain on corporate finances, and it is crucial to ensure good cashflow. The financial strength of a company is, however, not determined by cashflow alone. The ultimate criterion is the value of the company.

According to the shareholder value approach, developed in the 1980s, all activities should be geared to raising the share value, but this view is one-sided. The company cannot restrict its aims in the long term to maximizing value for a single interest group – the shareholders. As I have said before, corporate dynamism entails optimizing value for all interest groups. In practice there is not necessarily a conflict between the two approaches, since optimizing economic values in the shareholder value approach also genuinely raises value for most other stakeholders. When the company's finances are stronger, for example, employees can be better paid. The community profits from a higher tax revenue, and customers and suppliers like to deal with a healthy company. The dynamic companies we looked at have clearly shown that it is quite possible to obtain substantial increases in value for both shareholders and the other stakeholders.

Taking the broader stakeholder approach, however, it seems advisable to focus on the value of the company itself rather than on shareholder value alone. The activities introduced by management must contribute to raising the company's (long-term) value, an aim which will benefit both shareholders and other stakeholders. Clearly, though, the tools of the shareholder value approach can also be appropriate to the dynamic approach.

Alfred Rappaport refers to six 'value drivers' which can be used to maximize the company's value.[12] In simplified form, these are as follows:

1   Increased turnover raises operational cashflow.
2   Higher operational profit margins have a beneficial effect on cashflow.
3   If the profit/tax ratio can be improved by skilful tax accounting, cashflow will rise.
4   Reducing investment in working capital increases cashflow.
5   Reducing investment in fixed assets also increases cashflow.
6   A lower proportion of external capital will cut capital costs and make more financial resources available to the company.

These six 'value drivers' need to be carefully managed in the right direction to increase company value.

Two basic questions come to mind:

- How much additional shareholder value can be generated by developing new value potential? This should be a central financial criterion in judging value potential.
- What is the relationship between value potential and value drivers? This question was raised by my colleague, Peter Gomez, who suggests that any activity designed to develop value potential will affect the value drivers. This shows up more clearly in a matrix: Figure 5.6 uses the example of a wholesale distributor to show which measures could lead to an increase in the company's value. Of course every single measure needs to be carefully evaluated to assess the extent of its contribution to company value. The great advantage of this analysis is that the grid, bringing in the wider value potential view, makes it possible to identify and evaluate all the activities which could lead to an increase in value, without prejudice. Traditional programmes, by contrast, tend to be restricted to one specific value driver, as, for example, cost-cutting programmes to raise profit margins.

Would-be dynamic companies should start by finding out which activities that exploit value potential would also increase the value of the company. Concentrating on these activities will provide the highest benefits and give maximum leverage.

How to select value potential

The dynamic company develops precisely defined, attractive value potential by multiplying appropriate concepts. The choice of value potential

| | Value potential | | | | | |
Value drivers	Market potential	Procurement potential	Internal human potential	Information potential	Takeover and restructuring potential	etc.
Turnover growth	Better mix New kinds of offer	Backward integration Pooled purchasing	Incentives Training centre New type of salesman	Locking in customers, service New payment system	Foreign acquisitions	...
Cashflow, margin	Pricing policy Sales promotion Mix of range	Backward integration Purchasing marketing	Flexible working Opening times Training	Overhead value analysis Automation	Dismantling overheads Synergies	...
Investments Working capital Fixed assets	Space usage Sale and lease back	Investment/ divestment in production plant	Build up management capacity (strategic reserve)	Stock, creditor, debtor management Cash management	Purchase price	...
Capital costs	Gearing Disposal of superfluous assets	Gearing		Gearing	Gearing (share swopping)	...
Profit/tax ratio	Optimization of company structure	Optimization of company structure		Optimization of company structure	Optimization of company structure	...

Figure 5.6 *Increasing the value of the company by exploiting concrete value potential (using the example of a wholesale distributor). The company's value can be increased by value drivers.*

is therefore fundamental to entrepreneurial thought and action.

As we have seen, value potential goes through different stages, and the dynamic company must take care that its activities are geared to attractive value potential, that is to say, emerging or growing potential. With new value potential like this the choice simply involves assessing the potential and, if it holds sufficient promise, making a firm decision to concentrate on it. A company exploiting value potential which is already mature or declining, however, will have the more difficult task of targeting new value potential.

A consideration of the basic questions presented above should show up what value potential is open to the company and how attractive it is. Then the decision has to be made: What value potential is to be targeted? There may also be the question of whether to develop one kind of potential alone, or several at once.

Both extremes occur in practice: McDonald's directs all its activities exclusively to the market-related potential of fast food restaurants. At the other extreme, Nokia develops all the value potential it can find. Market-oriented business plans are put into practice by a strong research and development department. Restructuring potential is developed by taking over foreign competitors, combining and regrouping business activities and disposing of any inappropriate elements. The company also makes financial innovations in the form of new loans and human innovations in the shape of highly motivating personnel management schemes.

The Swiss firm Mikron has chosen a middle course. In the early 1960s this company, which generates stakeholder value in virtually every respect, was still a highly specialized manufacturer of cogwheel rolling mill machinery, with a turnover of a few million SFr. Even at that time the management recognized that the market potential for mechanical clocks, and hence for the machines used to make them, was maturing. They proceeded to develop new potential in a balanced and coherent way, by entering the market for transfer and later for universal milling machines. They diversified their expertise in microgearing into a new product line – technical precision parts in synthetic materials. Thus they increased turnover several times over. The company has also developed considerable financial potential in the Swiss capital market, and very recently has expanded its ability to restructure ailing machine manufacturers, with several successful takeovers and reorganizations.

There is of course no hard and fast rule which says whether it is right to follow one extreme or the other, or to steer carefully in between. The following criteria may help the decision in the individual case:

If an innovation holds great potential, then it would surely be wrong to dissipate energy, and the best results come from a concentrated multiplication of the concept. Sam Walton, owner of the very successful American chain Wal-Mart, concentrates on the attractive value potential of a new kind of discount store. In 1988 he opened nearly 150 new stores. In such a case simplicity should be the watchword.

Very often, however, no value potential presents itself as being singularly attractive. Here it is sensible to harness several different kinds of potential each of which exhibits some – if scarcely spectacular – attraction.

Sometimes it is difficult to estimate in advance the success of one specific kind of value potential. Here it is wise to tackle several kinds of value potential and try out the possible products or concepts. We could use military parlance and call this a 'reconnaissance in force' which should reveal where breakthroughs might be feasible.

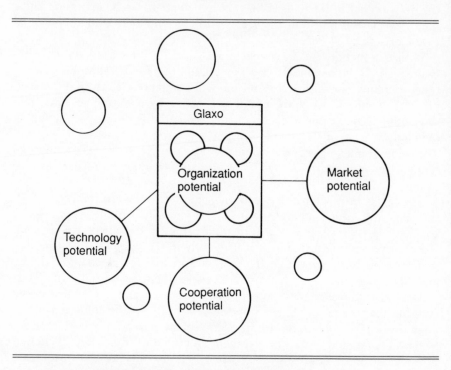

Figure 5.7 *Bundling of value potential by Glaxo*

A further point in favour of tapping into several different kinds of value potential is that it helps to spread the risks. If economic or other factors were to make one kind of value potential unproductive, there would still be other possibilities open to the company.

The constant development of a variety of potential can also be a good way to train entrepreneurial managers. Younger managers can learn how to implement projects in the real world.

In other words, if the company finds enormous potential which allows it to multiply extensively, then generally speaking it will be worth concentrating on this potential alone. In all other cases, it is advisable to develop a suitable combination or bundle of value potential in several fields, resulting in a mixture of activities. The different kinds of value potential can be given an order of priority. Figure 5.7 shows the bundle of potential developed by Glaxo.

Finding value potential which is good for the company is a continuous process which must never be put aside. The entrepreneur must be constantly on the alert for new value potential, especially when new moves are suggested, whether a takeover bid or a proposal for refinancing. In my assessment flexibility and openness are important characteristics of the dynamic company.

The energizing corporate concept

Establishing what value potential is to be developed is one of the most important decisions to be made, but it is only the foundation on which the company can build. The corporate concept contains the struts to take the building higher.

Firstly there must be a central idea, perhaps a slogan, which expresses the entrepreneur's philosophy or vision. Some examples are:

- 'Nobody knows the hamburger business better than we do.' (McDonald's)
- 'Führend in Anlageberatung' (leaders in investment consultancy) (Bank in Liechtenstein)
- 'Kommunikation ist unsere Aufgabe' (communication is our job) (Bertelsmann)

Secondly, strategic excellence positions (SEPs) must be defined. These are the specific abilities the company must acquire in order to develop value potential and assure its future.[13]

Thirdly, narrower strategies, specific to the chosen value potential, have to be worked out. Market potential requires market, product and innovation strategies. Company takeovers need acquisition strategies. Financial strategies are needed for potential in the capital markets, and other relevant strategies for internal value potential.

Corporate dynamism can also be generated by developing attractive value potential which lasts only one or two years, such as cost-cutting programmes or reorganizations. The dynamic corporate concept must take such short-term potential into account as well.

There is a wide variety of literature on concepts and strategies.[14] I shall highlight some aspects important to corporate dynamism:

One crucial point is that the company slogan, the SEPs and the individual strategies must form an organic and consistent whole. As Drucker puts it, every successful entrepreneur must have a theory of his company.[15] Practically all the dynamic companies we examined fulfilled this requirement and its importance was stressed in all our interviews. Dr Marc Wössner of Bertelsmann sees the clear concept behind his company as a major reason for its success.

Interestingly enough, many of the successful firms developing financial potential meet this criterion equally well. To the conventional eye Hanson plc appears to be a conglomerate involved in a variety of businesses. On closer analysis, however, it becomes clear that Hanson plc pursues an extremely clear corporate concept. Its central idea is to take over 'undermanaged companies' in basic industries and restructure them. These companies are not acquired at random but have to satisfy a strict catalogue of requirements as regards technology, their financial basis and the possibility of restructuring them. Hanson's particular ability (SEP) is its expertise in acquisition and restructuring, a process which it multiplies consistently and confidently.

What are the characteristics of a coherent, organic, corporate concept?

Firstly, there is a precisely formulated vision of the company's future. The main object of attack is unambiguously defined, and the direction of attack serves as a guideline for all activities.

Secondly, the strategies are harmoniously grouped around the central idea. Successful entrepreneurs make a point of cultivating harmony. Beat Curti, who has built up a company with more than one thousand million DM turnover, places particular stress on the aesthetic dimension. To him a company is like a work of art and should be beautiful, harmonious, coherent and expressive. (He even uses the analogy of nineteenth-century German opera and talks of a synthesis of the arts.) The innovative element is important as in art, where many famous artists, such as Rembrandt, Monet or Picasso, founded or helped to found new stylistic movements. Another factor is recursion: every little part reflects the basic structure of the whole, just as every cell in a set of chromosomes contains the code for the entire organism. The work of all important artists has this recursive quality. Think for example of the great J. S. Bach: you only need to hear a tiny excerpt from the Brandenburg Concertos to recognize the composer.

The same qualities can be expected of an organic company: the company has a certain beauty and is harmonious. The corporate concept is coherent and well balanced. The company expresses itself well (eg through a strong image). Furthermore, corporate development is based on innovative products, and the marks of the corporate concept are to be found in all parts of the company.

These ideas may seem strange in a sober financial and economic world, but it is surprising how many dynamic companies practise such principles.

IKEA and Bertelsmann, to name but two, deliberately cultivate this dimension. The costs of an organic organization need not be high: what matters is a good concept and the will to turn it into reality. IKEA, like any other trading company, tries to keep its building and running costs as low as possible, but none the less its shops have aesthetic appeal. On the walls of Habasit AG, a leading manufacturer of transmission and conveyor belts, are pictures painted by the workers themselves, one of the simple ways being used to decorate the workplace.

The aesthetic element has always played an important role in the history of mankind. Even Cro-Magnon man decorated the famous caves at Périgeux with works of art, and in the ancient cultures art stood at the centre of human creation. Why, then, should aesthetics be unimportant to the organization of a company?

There is, however, a clear distinction between surface cosmetics and aesthetics which express a deeply ingrained and harmonious concept.

Why is an organic corporate concept with clear strategic orientation so important to the dynamic company?

Firstly, a clear strategy reduces complexity. The company restricts its field of activities and becomes much simpler to manage:

- Concentrating on the chosen value potential means that much more can be learnt about it, and this increased knowledge leads to better decisions.
- With this depth of knowledge about the business, decisions will no longer be halfhearted, but will be confidently made and implemented.
- Tasks will be carried out quickly.
- Supervision is easier; mistakes are spotted sooner and can be quickly controlled.

No less important is the effect of the organic concept on the workforce and on some of the company's other stakeholders:

- The company's credibility, and that of its management, are proven. With a clear concept it is easy to understand what the management is doing and why.
- The character of the organic company is felt throughout because of its harmony, energy, power of expression and what we have called recursion, and this has a motivating effect.
- The clearly recognizable strategy and harmonious corporate concept give deeper meaning to the company's activities, resulting in genuine motivation.
- The organic company must be ethically irreproachable, if it is to remove any obstacles to its actions.
- The *unité de doctrine* which grows from the organic corporate concept is ultimately the basis of every strong culture.

A clear strategic orientation and an organic conception of the company are two mainsprings of dynamism. They create the basis for motivation, culture and a sense of purpose, factors which are becoming ever more important to success.

Flexibility v. continuity

Management theory since the 1960 has seen a threefold distinction between:

- Corporate policy or corporate strategy, which define the long-term direction of the company
- Planning and budgeting, which relate to the medium or shorter term
- Everyday management systems for the short term.

Is this a sensible division in the context of corporate dynamism? Let us look at two extremes.

- The world in which we are living is a turbulent one, where new situations, be they oil crises, stock market crashes, exploding (or slumping) property prices, or technological breakthroughs, arise very rapidly, bringing both dangers and opportunities. Existing value potential is eroded and new value potential is born. Generally speaking a dynamic company should exploit the value potential which yields the greatest benefits for its stakeholders, so that extreme flexibility is desirable: any value potential which presents itself is exploited in a creative and masterful, in other words a dynamic, way.
- On the other hand the strategic direction of the company calls for continuity and persistence. From this point of view the company should not keep jumping on bandwagons, but should steadfastly pursue the course drawn up in the strategy, ignoring short-term events. Establishing competitive positions takes considerable time. If the company changes direction too often, there may not be enough time to build up the skills for success. 'Cobbler, stick to your last' would be the guiding maxim for management of this kind.

Of course it is for every company to find its own ideal path between these two extremes. I should like simply to sketch out some principles which are relevant to dynamism:

Firstly, a turbulent business environment demands greater flexibility. 'Cobbler, stick to your last' can all too easily turn into 'Cobbler, die by your last'. For example, in the early 1970s NCR, the American cash register maker, was still concentrating on the production of electromechanical tills. Top management were oblivious to the speed with which fully electronic tills were taking over, and 'stuck to the knitting', to use the Peters and Waterman phrase. The market share for electromechanical cash registers fell from 90 per cent to 10 per cent between 1972 and 1976, and NCR had to write off over $100m. worth of obsolete cash registers.[16] Obviously in this case adherence to the strategic principles of persistence and reliance on existing strengths was misplaced. In such cases the development of new value potential should involve diversification, however hard this may be. Steady concentration of forces is only right when the value potential is still growing.

Secondly, some value potential, mainly internal potential such as cost-cutting, organizational or balance sheet potential, holds only short- or medium-term attraction. A loosely managed company may none the less find it well worth developing. Cost-cutting programmes, organizational unbundling or projects to reduce working capital are hardly strategic measures, but they can make a great contribution to the dynamic process.

Here lies the difference between the purely strategic approach and the dynamic approach: the dynamic approach is primarily concerned with the attraction of the value potential and requires value potential to be developed consistently both at the long-term, strategic, level and on the operational plane. Business activities are to be carried out within the frame of a harmonious corporate concept. The dynamic approach thus combines strategic and operational elements, while the strategic approach stresses the long-term direction. Dynamism thus allows, or even requires, much more flexible management. The strategic management model and the dynamic approach are contrasted in Figure 5.8.

Both approaches define the conceptual orientation of the company, but within this orientation strategic actions are geared more to the long term. Timescale is much less important in the dynamic approach, where attractive value potential can be flexibly exploited within the defined direction.

One way of increasing flexibility is to find new, greater value potential. Forbo, the leading flooring manufacturer in Europe, successfully pursued this strategy. In the 1970s and 1980s the regional floor and wall covering markets were quite mature, and concentrating exclusively on market strategies to increase market share could have brought only disappointing results. For this reason, in the late 1970s Forbo began to develop greater value potential by acquiring medium-sized wall and floor covering firms. This potential was still emerging at the time, as many company proprietors decided to offer their firms for sale as a result of the economic recession of the 1970s. The new takeover strategy made Forbo much more flexible: it entered a number of new markets, thus achieving a better balance. As it merged with other companies it gained a wider variety of ranges and marketing approaches and was able to make flexible use of the available management potential.

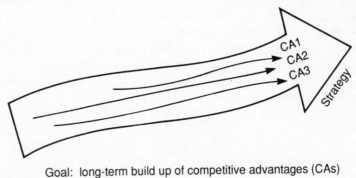

Goal: long-term build up of competitive advantages (CAs)

Figure 5.8a *The competitive strategy approach*

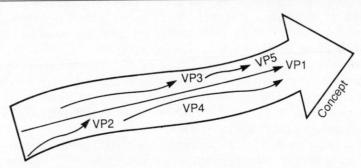

Goal: flexible (long- and short-term) exploitation of value potential

Figure 5.8b *The corporate dynamism approach*

It is useful to diverge from the paradigm of current management theory, which perceives the survival of the company as the overriding objective. There has been much discussion recently about whether this paradigm is still sustainable, or whether 'shareholder value' should not be seen as a more important goal. I find exclusive concentration on a single interest group, in this case the shareholders, nearly as problematic as the myth of the survival of the company. The highest goal must be perceived to be benefits for all stakeholders, which solves the problem of survival much more neatly. The company is seen as a productive social system which generates benefits for all stakeholders. Any given entity, such as a joint stock company, continues in existence only as long as this function is fulfilled. If other, more suitable kinds of benefit appear, then they should be preferred. I shall return to this theme in the Epilogue.

The company needs a clear concept, but there must be great flexibility within it. This means two things:

- Firstly the company must be able to adapt as quickly as possible to new directions. It needs the ability to learn.
- Secondly the company must keep an open mind. Total value of output (ie benefits for all stakeholders) takes priority over the continuation of present activities. If some of the relevant value potential is seriously eroded, then unconventional solutions will have to be found as soon as possible, while there is still room for manoeuvre.

In other words, managers must be able to think and act flexibly.

Guidelines for management

Moral precepts

The dynamic entrepreneur and manager regularly tests the moral precepts of the company, analysing carefully whether all stakeholders continue to profit from the company's output.

Basic questions

The dynamic principle raises a number of basic questions which must be objectively answered at frequent intervals. Most important, it must be established what phase has been reached by the value potential developed by the company and which activities the company is currently multiplying.

The organic total concept

Growth promoters define the value potential to be developed by the company in future. They cultivate an organic total concept of the company, distinguished by harmony, coherence, a sound ethical stance and suitable aesthetics.

Flexible exploitation of value potential

A volatile business environment means rapid changes in value potential. The dynamic manager is pragmatic and open-minded enough to develop new value potential flexibly and ruthlessly abandon outdated activities.

Notes

1   See Porter, 1985, p. 37.
2   See Abell, 1980, p.29.
3   Upper managers are specifically mentioned here because in many static companies they consciously or unconsciously maximize their own benefits. This is evident from the way everything they do is designed to defend their own position. Often unpleasant decisions such as restructuring are postponed. This escape from unpleasant decisions is in itself a benefit which top managers draw from the company.
4   We shall talk about this point in more detail later.
5   See for example Rappaport, 1986.
6   Levitt, 1960, pp. 45–56.
7   See eg Quinn, 1985, pp. 24–32; Peters, 1987, pp. 191ff.; Hinterhuber, 1984, pp. 88ff.; Foster, 1986; Goldsmith and Clutterbuck, 1985, pp. 160ff.
8   See Quinn, op. cit., p. 28.
9   See Ansoff, 1965, p. 109.
10 See Argenti, 1976, pp. 76ff.
11 See Whitney, 1987, pp. 49–55; Bibeault, 1982, pp. 203–307; Siegwart, Caytas and Mahari, 1988b.
12 Rappaport, op. cit., p.76.
13 See Pümpin, 1989.
14 See eg Pümpin, 1989; Hrebiniak and Joyce, 1984, pp. 2ff.; Vancil and Lorange, 1975, pp. 81–90; Lorange and Vancil, 1976, pp. 75–81.
15 Drucker, 1975, pp. 74ff.
16 Foster, op. cit., pp. 139ff.

Chapter 6

Structures: making space for dynamism

Embedding dynamism in the corporate constitution

The corporate constitution embodies the principles governing the way a company is run. It is documented in a number of places such as the Articles and Memorandum of Association and in any other statements of organizational or legal requirements. Our interest here is in those elements of the constitution of dynamic companies which lay the foundations for expansive development.

Once again Bertelsmann provides a perfect example. As early as 1960 Reinhard Mohn brought out an 'order of principles' including a number of constitutional standards. The first true company constitution was brought into force in 1973, and was amended in 1980.

The main principles embodied in Bertelsmann's corporate constitution are as follows:[1]

- The company must make a positive contribution to society;
- Within the company every effort will be made to assist all employees in achieving their full potential in the realm of work;
- Profit is the measure of productivity and a precondition for the continuation of the company. It is both right and necessary to pay interest on capital. Profit takes on a new quality with the involvement of employees in the company;
- A further objective is to contribute taxes, in order to facilitate the functions of the state;

• Finally every company – as well as holding classic political authority – has a social and political duty to influence economic policy.

The constitution contains several elements which are important to corporate dynamism, and in complete agreement with the philosophy of this book:

Firstly it rests firmly on the stakeholder approach which I advocate. The company has to harmonize the interests of its stakeholders.[2] It further stipulates that the benefits for all stakeholders are to be increased.

The company's employees are given a central role. Reinhard Mohn says elsewhere: 'So I advise the capital, in its own interests, to be ready to cooperate in the company and to understand the economic dynamism of a company in partnership.'[3] It is indeed fundamental to corporate dynamism that the workforce has a sense of identification and motivation. This can be obtained to some extent by assisting self-realization through training, making the workplace attractive and so on, but employee participation is a vital element too. It not only encourages employees to identify with the company, but also helps them to accumulate capital and thus provide for their old age.

Reinhard Mohn was perceptive enough to see the financial connection between participation and dynamic corporate expansion, a connection which should not be underestimated. Bertelsmann is dynamic because of its expansion: a middle-ranking company in 1948, with a turnover of 1m. DM and 350 employees, by 1987 it had developed into the largest media concern in the world, with a turnover of 9,200m. DM, and 42,000 employees. This powerful development was only possible because capital was raised steadily not least through employee participation, which thus brought many financial advantages to the company. Mohn stresses this quite clearly: 'The participation of the workers in profits in the early 1950s must not be seen simply as a social measure. Almost all of the company's profits were paid out to the workers, who then made them available to the company again in the shape of loans. ... At a time when the company could hardly raise capital for itself because of tax laws and difficulties in raising credit, it was thus able to finance the building up of the publishing business.'[4] And elsewhere: 'The company is increasingly financed by the workers' investments.'[5]

Bertelsmann is also a pioneer in other aspects of the corporate constitution, such as the composition of its supervisory board. Mohn secures the selection of independent, highly qualified members who can ably support the management.[6] Many companies overlook the influence of their non-executive directors, and all too often the tone of the board is set by bankers, big industrialists, trustees, lawyers and, not least, politicians. This inevitably results in conflicts of interest. The banker's primary concern is to ensure the security of the credit extended by his institution, and of continuing business for the bank. Trustees, lawyers and politicians are equally justified in stressing, respectively, the financial, legal and political aspects. They all want to minimize risks. Everything which is important to their interests is necessarily less important to corporate dynamism, and can even work against it. So dynamic companies stipulate in their constitutions that priority should be given, in the composition of upper management, to entrepreneurs. The great success of Swedish industry is attributable to the domination of the entrepreneurial element in Swedish supervisory boards.

The relationship between company and shareholders is also defined at constitutional level. A wide range of attitudes to shareholders is discernible, ranging from the 'shareholder value approach' of the USA to the perception of the shareholder in many European countries as a burden. The German banker Carl Fürstenberg is often quoted as having said: 'Shareholders are stupid and cheeky. Stupid, because they buy shares, and cheeky, because they want dividends as well.'

The objective of the dynamic approach – to create value for all stakeholders – invalidates both these extremes. The constitution of the dynamic company takes account of the legitimate interests of the shareholders, giving them useful, reliable information and a sensible dividend policy. In Switzerland and West Germany in particular there is still some way to go in this direction.

The constitution should keep organizational and management regulations to a minimum. I shall return to this topic later. Suffice to say for now that detailed regulations run counter to the principles of flexible adaptability, decentralization and autonomy which are essential to corporate dynamism.

The dynamic effect of a constitution framed in the right spirit is self-evident:

- As all stakeholders participate in the company, there is growing readiness to cooperate for the future.
- The employees take on a central position, which promotes their sense of identity with the company and their motivation.
- Employee participation is not only a way to improve motivation, but also assists in the financing of dynamic expansion, again involving all stakeholders.
- An enterprising board of directors works towards the prospective development of the company rather than safety and low risks.
- Capital investors can see the dynamics and are willing to make additional risk capital available in case of need.
- Bureaucratic regulations are confined to the necessary minimum.

Hence the constitution acquires a key role in dynamic development. If the wrong course is set at this level, the best intended dynamic efforts will come to nothing.

Self-management, flexibility and the ability to multiply: key factors in the dynamic organization

The problem of time

The development of dynamics is ultimately a question of skilful time management. There must be enough time at every level for expansionary activities. The time can be made by working twelve to sixteen hours a day, seven days a week, a practice which is quite often seen. The businessman struggles to cope with expansion on top of all his operational problems. The dangers of such behaviour are well known: the burden becomes too great to bear. I know of a case where this situation ended in suicide. It goes without saying that this makes a nonsense of dynamism.

In my interviews I was therefore always especially interested in those companies whose leaders were able to reduce their workload to a tolerable level and yet carried their company into new dimensions. A prime example is Klaus Jacobs. In 1975 the German company Jacobs AG had a turnover of 1,300m. SFr. In the 1987 business year Jacobs Suchard AG raised a turnover of 6,100m. SFr., and net profit has risen from 5.4m. SFr. to 265m. SFr. At the same time Klaus Jacobs was able to devote enough time to dressage to compete at world class, achieving an excellent second place in the European Championships in 1977, even though it was already difficult by then for anyone but *de facto* professionals to succeed at this level.

Other heads of dynamic companies also demonstrate that there are methods of keeping the workload at a sensible level. Robert Jeker finds the time, besides his successful and stressful work as President of the Schweizerische Kreditanstalt, both for the equally time-consuming role of colonel in command of a regiment of infantry and for regular, almost daily sport. Alain Dominique Perrin, head of Cartier, has a number of outside interests. He has succeeded in bringing together the quarrelling vintners of the Cahors wine region, where he has a chateau, and with their agreement has taken on the marketing of their little-known aromatic wines.

So it is certainly possible to generate dynamics without spending too much time on it. The shape of the organization plays a crucial role.

The entrepreneurs I have mentioned are able to limit the time they spend in the office because of the way the company is organized. However, growth promoters are intensely committed to the fortunes of the company. This is very important: it is not the number of hours worked that counts, but commitment to the expansionary objectives and the will to work for the future. Thus the growth promoter constantly brings fresh energy to the company with challenging goals, impulses and missions.

What are the organizational principles followed by dynamic entrepreneurs?

The tasks

The dynamic company needs an entrepreneurial manager to keep a constant eye on current or possible value potential. He or she will repeatedly review the questions presented earlier.

This will be the entrepreneurial manager's most intensive job. It requires thorough and careful thinking, but depends more on the quality of thought than on hours of work. The most productive thinking often occurs outside the office: it can happen at formal board or management meetings, but talking to friends or mentors, whether like-minded or critical, is just as important. It is also useful to break away from the daily round. Beat Curti, successful architect of the Hofer-Curti Group, gets away by walking in the mountains, sometimes for several weeks. Robert Jeker (as, incidentally, the author) turns to sport. Martin Hilti likes to think while out shooting, the shooting itself being less important than the distance from the office and the stimulation of the open air.

The entrepreneur can also help – as far as time allows – with operational activities. He or she can help to harness new value potential and to support multiplication. Any occupation with activities linked to mature or declining value potential, however, is mostly a waste of time. The enterprising manager should have nothing to do with it!

Autonomous subsystems

To enable the entrepreneurial manager to concentrate on the tasks outlined above, the operational emphasis should fall on the lower levels of management.[7] This means that the entrepreneur should have under him a number of autonomous subsystems with the following characteristics:

- Heading the subsystem is a manager with full operational responsibility for the relevant area. It is therefore crucial that the right person should be appointed at divisional or functional level, and that they should continue to be developed and encouraged.
- The leaders of the autonomous units must be able to be enterprising. They must be given wide-ranging authority to manage. Their motivation and commitment to the company must also be promoted, not only by the skilful use of incentives, but, increasingly, by employee participation.
- As tasks are widely delegated, they are rarely carried out directly by the person with authority and responsibility for them. However, the company needs to remain a cohesive entity, so indirect management elements such as the corporate culture grow in importance.
- Extensive delegation does not mean relinquishing control. There must be careful financial supervision.

We found organizational subsystems run along these lines in most of the dynamic companies we looked at. For example, in the early 1960s Mikron Holding AG, although only a small mechanical engineering firm, had already built up a holding structure with a turnover of 10m. SFr. Since then it has created a large number of autonomous units with completely independent operations. Klaus Jacobs, Chairman of Jacobs Suchard AG, sees autonomous subsystems as an absolute necessity if a company is to have international clout. This is what he said in an article in the *McKinsey Quarterly*:

> In looking at our business we found that we really make money at only two levels in the organization: at the very top, where we control resources and set policies and guidelines with respect to vital issues of commodities purchasing, currencies, and the like; and in the firing line, in our country-based product organizations. We resolved to concentrate our best management talent in the firing line, making those people responsible for the country-based business units and then ruthlessly stripping away as many as possible of the intervening management layers between them and top management in Zurich.[8]

Nowadays the concept of autonomous subsystems is gaining acceptability and is more commonly applied, though objections are still raised on the conservative side. Outdated traditional company structures are clung to 'because of the tax situation', which clearly obstructs dynamic development.

Some classic autonomous subsystems are subsidiaries, profit centres, divisions or business areas which are either fully integrated or under the complete control of the parent. The argument is too often put forward, particularly on legal grounds, that only a 100 per cent stake is acceptable. In some cases this argument is justified, but in future dynamic companies will find increasingly flexible forms of participation.

Some recent innovative organizational developments are gaining importance in the light of corporate dynamism:[9]

- *Greenhouse:* A greenhouse is the company's own holding company for internal business ventures, taking the role of a venture capitalist. It is a separate division with the task of promoting internal developments which either become profit sources for other areas of the business or develop into profit centres themselves.

- *Spinout:* A spinout is a cost centre which is separated out from the organization. In addition to its existing responsibility for costs, the spinout is given responsibility for profit, thus becoming a profit centre. American Airlines, for example, makes its training facilities available to other airlines, and its maintenance services can be used by private companies.

- *Yeastbuds:* A yeastbud is a team working on a project basis to expand divisional technologies, channel them into new products or penetrate new markets. If the project is successful the team may continue as a separate division, or it may be reintegrated. A yeastbud is widely autonomous: though controlled, it may be located far away from headquarters. One successful yeastbud is developing personal computers at IBM.

- *Skunk works:* A skunk works is a research and development unit segregated out from the organization and located outside the parent company. An 'outhouse culture' geared to innovation is deliberately cultivated by keeping control to a minimum and giving broad autonomy.

All these innovative organizations (which are as yet by no means uniformly described by the terms used here) are broadly detached from the routine of the company. They are therefore eminently suited to harnessing new value potential.

For autonomous subsystems to work best they should embrace all the major corporate functions, both the executive functions of development, production and sales, and ancillary functions such as accounting, personnel management and purchasing.

The boundaries of the system, especially with such organizations as spinouts or greenhouses, can be surprisingly flexible. New plans can only be successfully implemented if there are close relations between the company and other stakeholders such as suppliers and customers. Cooperation with research institutes and other sources of expertise is becoming more important. The boundaries of the system can thus be flexible in the following ways:

- The autonomous subsystem is often located away from the company, in the best conditions for the particular project. IBM's project to develop personal computers was completely detached from the main company, both organizationally and geographically, for example. A quasi autonomous subsystem, it was placed with the Entry Systems Division in Boca Raton, far from company headquarters in Armonk, New York. Freed from cultural and organizational restraints, the project took only eighteen months from development idea to introduction into the market.
- There are any number of variants in the financial control of

subsystems, ranging from 100 per cent control through a majority stake to a minority stake. Anyone who can contribute to the success of the project may be considered as a partner: third parties (suppliers, even competitors), specialist experts, and not least management and workforce.

The formation of autonomous subsystems removes a great burden from top management and gives executives the time they need to shape the future. It therefore helps to create the conditions for corporate dynamism. Tasks are divided in the following way:

- At the summit of the company entrepreneurs focus on activities linked to dynamism, such as finding and tapping into new value potential, and multiplication. Everything revolves around corporate expansion.
- The leaders of the autonomous subsystems concentrate on running operations as well as possible.

Greater dynamism can be achieved by focusing on new value potential and multiplication not only at the top level, but also lower down. In this case the subsystems are so-called autopoietic systems, able to reproduce themselves.[10] The dynamics begin to snowball. Bertelsmann and Electrolux both follow this model. At Bertelsmann the central board plans and initiates major acquisitions and other key projects. To use our terminology, value potential is developed in new business activities, and also in takeovers and restructuring. The same activities take place at divisional and profit centre levels. The heads of every section are expected to develop new value potential. Both divisional and profit centre leaders have to run their work in such a way that – as in our model above – there is enough time for dynamic expansion. Thus Bertelsmann has created a large number of entrepreneurs, all occupied with the development of the company at different levels of the hierarchy. Electrolux has a similar philosophy. Here too the initiative for taking over other white goods firms comes not only from the top level. Every national company is encouraged to exploit all the relevant possibilities for itself.

It is clearly far from easy to set up and manage an autopoietic system like this. The momentum unleashed on every level can be very dangerous and must be kept under strict control. On the other hand any control is detrimental to entrepreneurialism. It is no mean task for top management to find the right balance.

Flexibility

Why is flexibility so important to dynamism?

The main reason is doubtless the turbulence of the business environment which I have mentioned so often. Because change is difficult to forecast, companies are often confronted by unexpected developments. Flexible firms can make better use of the opportunities opening up and can more quickly deflect the dangers.

Change may result from the competition doing something unexpected, or from customer reaction being difficult to calculate. Some products become huge successes in the market, in spite of a very critical reception from the experts. Take 3M's 'Post it', for example:

In the late 1960s 3M chemist Spencer Silver was experimenting with a polymer with adhesive properties. His trials produced a new adhesive which could be removed and reused. The management of 3M saw no great future for the adhesive and support for Silver's research was gradually withdrawn between 1968 and 1973. Then, by chance, a colleague hit upon the idea of applying the adhesive to pieces of paper and using them as sticky notes. Thanks to Silver's untiring commitment to 'selling' his invention internationally and to the support of some of his colleagues, the sticky notes were test marketed in 1978. The results were very disappointing and the project seemed dead. A few promoters, though, were not prepared to give up so soon, and the product was test marketed again, in San Francisco. At last the new product was proved to be a useful one, and the fabulous success of the yellow 'Post it' notes was born.[11]

Conversely, products developed with extreme care by experts and hailed as future market leaders have been known to fail dismally. The Ford Edsel is one example:

Ford launched the 'Edsel' in the autumn of 1957. Nothing had been left to chance: the model was conceived on the basis of motivation and market research, and the design team made over 4,000 separate decisions to ensure that the car was everything the customers wanted. It was given the name of the then CEO, Edsel Ford. But sales in 1958 were extremely sluggish, and the Ford Edsel was a marketing fiasco which cost the Detroit motor company around $350m.[12]

Dynamic companies can quickly exploit any opportunities which arise, but only because they are flexible. The German marketing strategist Meffert differentiates three kinds of flexibility:[13]

- Flexibility of action determines how much room there is for manoeuvre within the company. For example, production facilities should be able to be used in many ways; or there should be different sources of supply, so that raw materials and so on can be purchased quickly and easily.

- Process flexibility determines how quickly the company can react to change, because of skilful planning, decision making and implementation. Process flexibility can be increased for example by early warning systems or contingency planning.
- Structural flexibility defines how well organizational structures, personnel and management systems can absorb new developments. Nowadays increasingly flat structures, small organizational units and broad training are needed.

At first sight it may seem desirable to embrace all these types of flexibility. Unfortunately this entails certain disadvantages. Flexibility has a price: even in these days of CAD/CAM, flexible production facilities are expensive. Early warning systems and contingency plans are not cheap either, because staff have to be employed to take care of them. Small details often mean that economies of scale cannot be properly exploited.

The strategic implications, however, can be even more dramatic. One primary objective of strategic management is to attain competitive superiority in the form of strategic excellence positions (SEPs). The skills necessary for SEPs can only be built up if a company channels more energies (in the form of broader training, for example, or development of specialist expertise) into a strategic field of activity. Concentration of energy, however, works against flexibility: flexibility of action, for example, will be reduced by highly specialized production facilities, and process and structural flexibility will also be affected. At McDonald's, the concentration of energies in fast food restaurants restricts flexibility in many ways. What would happen to this company if the demand for fast food were unexpectedly to die down? It would be very hard to change production facilities or purchasing (no flexibility of action). Process flexibility would be restricted by the firm's distinctive 'hamburger culture', and rapid structural alterations would be difficult because the franchise agreements and other organizational systems are specifically geared to fast food restaurants.

It appears, then, that greater flexibility goes hand in hand with greater uncertainty about value potential. The management of McDonald's assumes that its value potential is still strong, so that it can concentrate on multiplying one type of restaurant. Obviously this is a very risky strategy. Allgemeine Treuhand (ATAG), a leading Swiss firm linked to Arthur Young International and specializing in audits and management services, found itself in quite a different situation in the early 1970s. Since then it has pursued a strategy of flexible expansion, consistently widening its range of services. Within the last fifteen years its business consultancy has been greatly strengthened, and it has built up a section handling business information, two measures which have increased turnover and profits eightfold. Extending the programme has led to much greater flexibility of action and processes.

Generally speaking very few firms nowadays are in the happy position of McDonald's. In many sectors the value potential is maturing or in decline, and finding new value potential is a constant challenge. Firms in this situation need to be very flexible. What does this entail?[14]

Flexibility of action requires diversity in purchasing, development, production and sales. Different sources of materials, broadly based development programmes, production facilities which can be used in many ways and a variety of sales channels should all be seriously considered.

Process flexibility calls for rapid reactions, both decisions and actions. Delegating the authority to take decisions is one way to speed them up; another is a simple decision making procedure. Small teams working closely and informally together are one possible solution.

Structural flexibility is particularly important to corporate dynamism. Flat organizational structures, small units, the minimum of bureaucratic regulations (job descriptions, etc.) are the order of the day. But the most important ingredient for flexibility is people with the right attitude. Every company needs versatile personnel.

To begin with, the board and management should be heterogeneous bodies representing a wide spread of educational and career backgrounds, age, nationality, and – increasingly – gender.

But more than this, every single manager and every employee should be trained in many ways, both in the workplace and at seminars. Many successful firms find job rotation a useful training tool, though it can vary widely from firm to firm. One large concern prides itself on the fact that on average managers change jobs every five years, while at Shell the international management is rotated every two to three years, often from one continent to another. The record is surely held by Club Med, whose Chefs de Village and GOs (*gentils organisateurs* – their representatives in the holiday villages) are relocated every six months, very often in completely different countries and continents. The Chef de Village bears full responsibility for the holiday village from the day he or she arrives, which represents an enormous challenge in view of the different national customs, languages and cultures, as well as personal networks. The costs of transporting over 6,000 employees long distances twice a year are enormous, but even so Gilbert Trigano, the Président Directeur-Général, is convinced of the necessity for rapid rotation. A few years ago an annual rotation was tried out on cost grounds, but with disastrous results: it transpired that after six months in the same place staff quickly became stale.

All in all, then, dynamic companies need to be flexible in order to identify and properly exploit value potential.

The ability to multiply

Dynamic companies expand by developing and multiplying organizational concepts. At Four Seasons Hotels, for instance, the organizational structure of the regional hotels is predefined and multiplied. The successful Swiss restaurant chain Mövenpick similarly multiplies predefined structures and processes in its restaurants.

But multiplying activities means standardizing them, which conflicts with flexibility. What is the answer?

One approach is to predefine only those factors which are vital to the whole concept. System multiplication will depend, for example, on a fixed layout for shops, restaurants or factories, on corporate and visual identity, on rules governing the fabrication of the product and on (financial) reporting systems. Many companies also prescribe strict quality standards. Expansion is achieved by multiplying these standardized structures and procedures. Flexibility and motivation are ensured by allowing the heads of the organizational units to use their own enterprise and initiative in other areas.

At the top of the company some other organizational measures can be multiplied. Legal forms can be standardized, for example – every Metro-Markt in West Germany is an independent legal entity – as well as accounting and consolidation. Standardization at this level should, however, go only as far as is absolutely necessary.

I should like to reiterate the importance of simple systems and regulations. Simple organizational concepts are much easier to multiply than highly complex models.

The dynamic organizational concept

It is already clear that the right organizational concept can support dynamics in many ways:

- The creation of autonomous subsystems under able management is a sensible way of releasing the top management of the company from operational duties. The entrepreneur and his closest colleagues gain the time they need to shape the dynamic expansion.
- Delegating duties, authority and responsibility downwards to the heads of the autonomous subsystems motivates them, which also promotes dynamics.
- Ideally the subsystems will also be dynamically managed, with those responsible for them occupying themselves primarily with dynamic development in their area and delegating operational duties further. The dynamics are multiplied.
- In many firms great flexibility encourages dynamism, allowing

opportunities to be taken quickly and unbureaucratically.

- However, where great value potential is being tapped by multiplication, the elements and processes which are vital to success must be standardized. The better organized these elements are, the easier it will be to multiply and thus generate dynamics.

Since dynamism can so obviously be increased by organizational measures, why do so many companies find it difficult to make the necessary changes? There are a number of reasons:

- Firstly, many able managers do not have the natural inclination to find and develop new value potential. They find such activities too risky and uncertain, and prefer to carry out the more familiar routine tasks. Such people are quite unwilling to make time available for expansionary activities.
- Secondly, the creation of autonomous subsystems means that top managers have to hand over power, and many are not prepared to do this.
- Thirdly, the concept of autonomous subsystems only works well when they are managed by very competent, enterprising managers. Such managers command high basic salaries and discretionary payments such as bonuses, incentives, profit sharing. Many companies will not pay enough.
- Fourthly, management often thinks that the company could achieve the same results in its existing form. It prefers not to disrupt departments which in many ways are working well in order to embark on a dynamic reorganization fraught with uncertainty.

Obstacles of this kind can of course bring the whole dynamic process to a standstill: because no one in the company takes any interest in new value potential, business is confined to the existing mature or already declining activities. In this situation the company can pour so much effort into working and motivating the staff that it becomes completely exhausted.

So every entrepreneurial manager must consider very carefully the questions I have raised. The key question, which needs a good honest answer, is: Are there any of these obstacles to dynamism in my company? Shareholders and directors should also be looking at this question.

Guidelines for management

Constitution

It is at the constitutional level that the structures are created which make it possible to manage dynamically. Greater attention must be paid to the interests of all stakeholders, to employee participation, to the appointment of entrepreneurial directors and to the abandonment of bureaucratic regulations.

Self-management

Autonomous subsystems should be set up, headed by enterprising managers who will develop their own dynamics. This will make your own job simpler and give you more time for expansionary tasks.

The development of the right managers for these autonomous subsystems is an important task for management.

Organizational forms

Make use of innovative and unconventional organization forms such as spinouts and greenhouses.

Flexibility

As the phases of value potential become shorter so flexibility is becoming ever more important, especially for companies whose value potential is in its later stages. These companies must increase flexibility of action, procedures and structures. Employee flexibility must also be encouraged.

Obstacles

Many firms are hampered by existing structures and systems, such as pay structures. You should have the courage to overcome these obstacles and try new ways.

Notes

1   See Biedenkopf, 1985, p.381.
2   In his book *Erfolg durch Partnerschaft* (Success through partnership) Reinhard Mohn repeatedly stresses the importance of this harmonization. See Mohn, 1986.

3   Ibid., p.142.
4   Ibid., pp. 54 ff.
5   Ibid., p. 73.
6   Ibid., p.39.
7   See de Woot, 1984, pp. 71ff.
8   Jacobs, 1987, p.50.
9   See Hanan, 1987, pp.40 ff.
10 See Probst, 1981, pp.306ff.
11 See Nayak and Ketteringham, 1987.
12 See Berg. 1971, pp. 2 and 228.
13 Meffert, 1985, pp.121ff. Meffert groups these three kinds of flexibility under the heading of 'Handlungsflexibilität' (flexibility of manoeuvre) and deals with other kinds of flexibility as well which are of less interest to us here.
14 See also ibid., pp. 126ff.

Chapter 7

Man-management: the touchstone of dynamism

The workforce – a company's most valuable asset?

Virtually every company report or management book you pick up today makes the point that people are the most valuable asset in the company. It is a straightforward thesis: after all, it is people – executives and workers – who perform the activities of the company. If they do not do their jobs well, then the company's existence is threatened. It is quite natural that the importance of the workforce should be highlighted in the literature.

Actual practice, however, is quite different, and not only in static companies. A great many very successful, dynamic, firms have a cold, authoritarian atmosphere. Superficial observation might even seem to support the theory that many major successes have only been possible thanks to an almost tyrannical entrepreneur. Some industrial pioneers, such as Rockefeller and Ford, have been extremely domineering. Contradictory examples, however, such as Thomas Watson Jr, Bob Hewlett and Gottlieb Duttweiler, immediately spring to mind. So what is the truth about people-orientation? Does it help or hinder dynamism? Does it make any difference at all?

These questions are easy to answer with reference to value potential. If considerable potential has been found and all it needs is to be developed by multiplication, then people-orientation can be of minor significance. Henry Ford developed powerful value potential with his Model T and his conveyor belt technique, and cars were practically torn out of his hands. In such a situation there are distinct advantages to authoritarian leadership:

clear, rapid decision making speeds up multiplication and makes good use of the learning curve and other beneficial effects.

The same example, however, also illustrates the problems of authoritarian leadership. When the value potential of the black Model T began to diminish because of technological progress – General Motors invented and introduced the Fisher body – Henry Ford was not in a position to react adequately. In fact, he fired several directors who confessed to thinking that Ford needed a change of policy. Ford's market share fell from 55.4 per cent in 1921 to 10.6 per cent in 1927. The company was on the brink of ruin.

Our analyses have shown that value potential rarely goes on growing for a long time. It is bound to mature and decline – sooner than ever, today. With such rapid evolution the company's success depends on the development of new value potential. And here even the authoritarian entrepreneur relies on the constructive contributions of the people around him – executive and non-executive directors as well as employees.

Of course the authoritarian entrepreneur will be very unwilling to admit his need for support. Has he not already proved that his methods are successful? Did he not personally recognize the value potential and develop it with great success? Such uncritical, retrospective questions as these are the stuff of many tragedies. The entrepreneur convinces himself that his success to date springs entirely from his personal ability to recognize value potential and his own performance as a leader of the multiplication process. His egocentricity is his undoing, for he does not realize that his success depended largely on exogenous factors such as the value potential he discovered, and that he may not be so fortunate again.

So, corporate dynamism can be achieved, temporarily at least, without an orientation towards people. In the long term, though, an authoritarian attitude is sure to lead to a dead end. Cases such as that of ITT after Geneen even lead me to say that the longer the autocratic phase lasts the harder it will be to revive the dynamic forces. For long-term corporate dynamism, management must reflect the needs of people.

Man-management in the dynamic company

Dynamics through trust

The flexibility and widespread autonomy which are essential to dynamic development can only evolve where there is a climate of trust among the executives and between management and workforce. Mutual trust gives executives the freedom and motivation to develop dynamics at all levels. It is not easy to build trusting relationships.

The company must have a philosophy which is shared without reservation by all its employees. *Unité de doctrine* promotes a feeling of identification with the company and of motivation. Only positive social attitudes and a sound ethical stance will endure. Once again we see the connection between dynamism and ethics.

Delegation based on trust means that often jobs will not be carried out in the way the superior intended. Mistakes can occur. It is part of a trusting organization that mistakes are accepted, within reasonable limits. Performance is judged not on mistakes, but on positive contributions to development. The culture of the dynamic company will always emphasize the positive and play down the negative.

The trusting organization uses these methods to create harmonious relationships between all employees. Teamwork is very important, with the achievement of the team mattering more than individual performance. There is no place here for the 'macho' manager.

Dynamics through communication

One way of cultivating trust is through open communications. Comprehensive information helps to improve problem solving, and motivation and identification are high in a transparent, accessible organization.

All kinds of communication should be encouraged. Oral communication, from one-to-one interviews to conferences and seminars, still plays a central role. No less important, however, are written and, more recently, electronic communication.

Dynamic companies take every opportunity to foster communication. There is the well-known coffee corner at Hewlett-Packard, which is used quite deliberately as an instrument of communication. Digital Equipment has a special 'Electronic Conferencing System' to which all its professional employees all over the world are connected. Every participant can feed questions into this system and within a few days will receive answers and tips from the experience of colleagues who have been faced with similar problems. The contribution of this system to problem solving is self-evident.

Finally, communication encourages flexibility. Employees inevitably learn more about other activities within the company, and can be employed in a wider range of different ways, to the benefit both of the company and of the individual's personal development. In addition it is easier to see how the company is run, and the whole organization can benefit from the learning experience.

The dynamic company communicates everything imaginable. It is important to supply regular information about the vision and purpose of the company, as well as about its strategic excellence positions. This promotes and gives substance to the corporate identity.

Dynamics through managing managers

The management of managers is a thorny subject. Dynamic companies face two fundamental problems: Firstly they need highly qualified executives who can take on new roles to assist with expansion. Secondly, their managers must always be able and willing to achieve the high level of performance they demand.

So the first consideration is the development of top managers. Formal training can be arranged both within the company and outside. It is much more important, however, for managers to learn entrepreneurial behaviour, and this cannot really be formally taught. It is better to learn on the job. Younger executives should be confronted with real-life problems as early as possible. They should be given positions where they can resolve issues for themselves, though of course there must be a competent senior manager – a mentor – to guide them. Intensive job rotation, where possible, will make them more flexible.

The second problem is rather more difficult. For a variety of reasons a manager may no longer be able to cope with the demands of the dynamic company: he or she may not get on with their superior, there may be problems in the team, or perhaps even trouble at home, or they may simply be too old. Sometimes the employee cannot fit in with the culture of the company. Cases like these occur relatively often: one very dynamic company had to refill over 70 per cent of its key positions in the space of three years.

The overriding aim in replacing employees is to ensure the continued atmosphere of trust within the organization. This means treating the outgoing manager with scrupulous fairness, both psychologically and financially.

Psychologically, the departing manager must not lose face and should on no account be branded a failure. There are always bound to be competent, expert executives who are absolutely loyal to the company but for some reason or other can no longer keep up the pace, especially in dynamic companies with their expansionary thrust. Their failure to perform does not by any means imply general incompetence. The dynamic company is aware of this fact and finds exit routes which suit the personal needs of its executives and keep their image untarnished. The job holder should also be able to expect a fair financial settlement which will allow him to fulfil his personal commitments and maintain his current lifestyle.

Ideally there should be no need to dismiss executives as they get older. Both in Japan and in progressive Western companies top executives are increasingly released from stressful operational management some years before official retirement. Hilti, for example, has developed a scheme for directors to leave the board at 55. The responsibility for production is passed on to a younger executive, while the ex-director takes on special projects or joins the supervisory board of a subsidiary company. This solution brings two advantages: Firstly young, 'hungry' executives can climb the ladder more quickly, instead of finding the way barred and having to look elsewhere. This is a great source of motivation for them. Secondly, the knowledge and experience of the older executives is retained within the company, where they can help with expansionary activities. But it can be difficult to implement such a regimen. It means that senior managers have to relinquish power, which, in Western countries, often implies a drop in status. The time has come for a more generous and less dogmatic culture!

An executive overstretched by dynamism could perhaps be moved to a position within the company which imposes less physical and mental pressure, say, in training or public relations.

Dismissing a manager is the hardest task of all. Perhaps the expected level of performance is no longer being achieved, or maybe the executive has become set in his ways. Many executives lack the mental vigour to rethink in line with strategic reorientations.

Here too the company must above all be fair to the executive, giving full support through the whole dismissal process. One well-known firm puts just as much time into this process as into appointing new managers. Executives may be channeled into new positions, say in the civil service or in politics, which are more prestigious though less dynamic.

Dynamics through training

The importance of training and education has already been mentioned. There are several good reasons:

- In the current economic climate companies need high expertise potential in order to succeed. Dynamic companies multiply highly developed processes or systems, and the knowledge that goes into these must constantly be developed further and passed on to other employees. Training plays a central role.
- Training assists communication within the company. The informal networks which are set up through training help to make the company more flexible and dynamic.
- Vocational training is positively motivating, since workers feel that the company is willing to develop their knowledge and skills.
- Finally, training can be used to shape cultural values. I shall be dealing with this aspect in more detail later.

This brief overview gives an idea of the importance of training. Certainly it is vital to dynamism that the staff should be extremely knowledgeable and highly skilled.

Dynamics through multiplying talents

Often there are outstanding talents within a company which never come to light because of bureaucracy, frustration and apathy. As bureaucracy is dismantled and motivation schemes are introduced, this internal human potential is unleashed, and can gradually be transferred to other areas of the business.

This concept is successfully applied by Forbo, the leading European manufacturer of floor and wall coverings, which has taken over a number of other, bureaucratic and unprofitable, firms in the same field. One of the first steps after every acquisition was to find out where there was expertise and how to release it. The company is most concerned to interchange, and give full play to, all the expertise it has, multiplying it into as many areas as possible.

This policy can of course be carried out not only in takeovers but in other dynamic measures as well.

Dynamics through incentive schemes

Corporate dynamism needs a high level of commitment from all the company's employees, and this commitment must be suitably rewarded. Incentive schemes are particularly important, but should not be confined to financial incentives. Non-financial incentives which express the company's appreciation and hence underline the high social status of the employee within the company represent a more important principle.

How should incentive schemes work?

- Firstly, incentives should be related not only to quality and/or quantity. Speed is just as important to corporate dynamism, so time should increasingly be seen as a criterion for the allocation of incentives.
- Secondly, share options are gaining significance as an addition to bonuses and awards, since they also help employees to identify with the company.
- Thirdly, new, creative incentives should be developed regularly, for incentive schemes become less effective as they lose their novelty value. Imaginative incentives, which need not be expensive, can result in surprisingly strong motivation.

Incentive schemes can only function properly when employees know that their performance is being objectively assessed. It is therefore sensible for management controls to generate data on details which are relevant to the dynamic process. Personal computers can take on the drudgery without great expense.

Dynamics through culture

It has long been recognized that corporate culture has a decisive effect on the behaviour of both executives and the workforce as a whole.[1] Most publications on the subject, though, take a psychosocial or strategic angle, and little attention has been paid to the particular cultural characteristics of dynamic companies. Our analysis shows that four basic orientations prevail in a dynamic corporate culture:[2]

- *Expansion-orientation:* Management and workers have a positive attitude towards growth. Ambitious goals for growth are set, and accepted. For example, the executives of Glaxo whom we interviewed showed great pride in the high rates of growth they had achieved.
- *Speed-orientation:* Time is valued as an important resource. Project deadlines are made deliberately tight, and a sport is made out of setting new records for speed. For example, Metro has repeatedly beaten its own records for the construction of its cash-and-carry stores. The store in Graz was opened about three months after the foundation stone was laid. The store in Hamburg was reopened one month after a serious fire: some customers, expecting a fire-damaged building, were astonished to find a completely intact new store. When I went to see Kari Kairamo at Nokia, I noticed large gumboots in various offices in the headquarters. Asked what they were for, Kairamo answered: 'Those are our seven-league boots, so that we can run even faster'! A speed culture affects many details: telephone calls are returned within minutes; enquiries are dealt with the same day; decisions are reached in the shortest possible time. It goes without saying that such a speed culture needs the right conditions and systems and constant attention in order to flourish.
- *Productivity-orientation:* Productivity standards are especially high in multiplicative activities. At Hanson for instance acquisitions are made by small but very productive teams. The headquarters of the £7,000m. company is not heavily staffed, with seventy employees including secretaries and ancillary staff. This orientation towards productivity is carried directly into the firms it takes over. Superfluous management levels are removed and operations are made very much tighter.
- *Risk-orientation:* Dynamic expansion needs enterprise, which, in a free

market economy, is inherently risky. The readiness to take risks and accept failures is another feature of the culture of dynamic companies.

Placing the emphasis on these four basic concerns is not without its consequences.

How do these four orientations fit in with the orientations which are more usually considered: customers (customer respect etc.), workforce (respect for employees, trust, teamwork, etc.), innovation (willingness to try things out, unconventional solutions, etc.), company (identification with the company, loyalty etc.) and technology (fitting in with specialist technology, etc.)?[3]

No company can achieve a high profile in all possible orientations. A culture is created by actions, and if these actions are distributed equally over all orientations, then the watering can principle takes effect: every orientation receives only a sprinkle, and they all level off fairly low. A strong profile comes only with a bias in the culture-forming activities.

It follows that companies strong in the four basic orientations outlined above are often weak in other basic orientations. This was borne out in the firms we looked at: some could not be said to have a strong customer-orientation, and others have no real cost-orientation. There is often – as we have already seen – little employee- and company-orientation, and often technology-orientation is neglected.

There can be great difficulties when static companies become dynamic. Their historical development, often over several decades, leaves a sharp imprint on their corporate culture, perhaps in the form of extreme sensitivity to costs, or an overnourished bureaucracy. In such cases going dynamic inevitably means a cultural reorientation towards expansion, speed, productivity and risk-taking, as described above.

A change in culture is an extremely demanding challenge for management. There will need to be a great many training seminars, workshops, communications and symbolic gestures.[4] It will have to be seen in each case whether the change can be made with the existing management. Examples such as Iacocca's reorientation of Chrysler or Jan Carlzon's transformation of SAS indicate that often it takes a new chief executive to initiate fundamental change.

Motivation: empty slogan or success factor?

Corporate dynamism can only be sustained in the long term if it is supported by a competent and motivated workforce. Everything will have some influence on employee motivation, and the dynamic company will try to ensure the continued commitment of its workforce in the following ways:

The company's personnel must have the right attitude. No amount of investment in training and development will help if the general attitude is not right.

A high priority must be given to the extensive use of all available motivational instruments.

Guidelines for management

People-orientation

Sustained dynamics need managers to have a people-orientation on which all their actions are based.

Man-management

The entrepreneurial manager's man-management fosters dynamism. He or she builds a solid foundation of trust and practises regular open communication. Managers are sensibly and fairly employed. Continual training is provided and expertise is transferred in a multiplicative way. Innovative incentive systems promote motivation.

Corporate culture

Dynamic companies have a distinctive corporate culture with four dominant features:

- Expansion-orientation
- Speed-orientation
- Productivity-orientation
- Risk-orientation

The dynamic manager sets an example and encourages the relevant standards and attitudes.

Notes

1   See Deal and Kennedy, 1982, pp. 13ff., Bleicher, 1989, pp. 40ff.; Kobi and Wüthrich, 1986, pp. 28ff.; Pümpin, 1984, p. 17.

2   By a basic orientation we mean a distinguishing feature of the corporate culture which is explicitly expressed in the company. See also Kobi and Wüthrich, op. cit., pp. 89ff.

3   On the terminology see Pümpin, 1985.
4   On the formation of culture see Kobi and Wüthrich, op. cit., pp. 155ff.

Chapter 8

Time: the critical resource

At the very beginning of this book we said that dynamic companies were those which could increase the benefits for their stakeholders *within a relatively short time*. This chapter enlarges on the close relationship between dynamism and time and highlights its implications for the management of the dynamic company.

The relationship between corporate dynamism and time is not altogether straightforward. It is not a simple matter of carrying on as before, only faster. The aim should be to accelerate the entrepreneurial process by running it more intelligently. Similarly, acceleration at the wrong moment is pointless. Good timing is crucial.

Dynamics need to be sparked off by an entrepreneurial manager, a growth promoter, whose job it will also be to stoke the fires of dynamic management and keep up the momentum. These are time-consuming tasks. Entrepreneurs and executives will only be able to carry them out satisfactorily if good time management releases them from other, less relevant, duties.

Management time for expansionary tasks

Time management has recently come into fashion. Everyone is offering seminars on the subject. There are a number of different approaches: Tom Peters and others recommend 'Management by wandering around', where the bulk of the time is spent outside the office in direct contact with customers and employees. Other authors let executives set their own priorities and merely compare the actual use of their time against them. It remains largely unclear what criteria should be used in setting priorities.

So, how should time be managed in a dynamically developing company? It was evident that the companies we looked at did not apply simplified standard prescriptions such as 'time for customer contact', but set totally different priorities. For example, the top management of Mikron, the mechanical engineering group, is very much oriented to 'wandering around' with the customers. Hanson, while just as dynamic, is exactly the opposite and frowns on 'wandering around'.

It is certainly not satisfactory for management to set haphazard priorities. Often executives simply give priority to jobs which they enjoy because they feel secure in them.

The right way must be to spend time on those activities which are most important to the corporate strategy. In other words, the strategy should act as a guideline for the management of time.[1] The dynamic company's strategy is to develop attractive value potential by multiplying business activities, and that is what the entrepreneurial manager should be spending time on – as long as the value potential is emerging or growing. If it is maturing or in decline then priority should be given to the search for new value potential.

There are, then, quite clearcut rules on time management in the dynamic company. Growth promoters, unlike the managers of static companies, consciously devote most of their available time to activities which allow considerable expansion. They delegate all other jobs. This is how to achieve the leverage we have talked about: it takes very little effort to roll a boulder if that effort is concentrated at the right point – on attractive value potential.

Leaders of static companies tend for one reason or another to waste their time on value potential which is already mature or declining. For example, one well-known businessman was reluctant to give up his personal contact with longstanding clients. He had become firm friends with some of them, and one was even the godfather of one of his children, so understandably he preferred to spend his time with them even when the relevant value potential was well into decline. Other similar factors are habit, familiarity, fear of the new and so on.

Becoming dynamic can be a wrench. Precious long-running relationships have to be abandoned and unfamiliar new jobs have to be tackled. It is hardly surprising that top managers who have mapped out a comfortable future for themselves avoid reorientations of this kind and prefer to spend time on jobs which may hold less promise but are all the more pleasant and secure.

Timing – more haste, less speed

Devoting most of one's time to finding and developing new value potential, assuming that the entrepreneurial manager is prepared to do it, is still no guarantee of future success. The secret is to act at the right time.

Timing is especially important when dealing with new value potential. AEG's launch of the video disc in the 1970s was obviously too early. So were Xerox's first ventures into desktop publishing, also in the 1970s. On the other hand – and this tendency is likely to grow from now on – value potential can be developed too late. The 'strategic window',[2] that is, the best period to launch a new product or service, is only open for a limited time, and it is up to you to hit the right moment. The question is: how?

On the one hand intuition is important. Leysen regards the feeling for the right moment as one of the three most important characteristics of the entrepreneur.[3] It must be said, though, that ultimately every feeling is based on experience.

On the other hand, strong indications of the right time to act can often be gleaned from conclusive information, which, while readily available, is not often picked up. Take President Reagan's deregulation policy. In the early 1980s the effects of the deregulation policy, which changed value potential in all kinds of markets, were mentioned in the press almost every day, but surprisingly few companies took the opportunities which arose.

High pressure performance

Dynamism is very closely linked with speed of action. Becoming dynamic always means speeding things up. Why?

We have established that attractive value potential is essential to corporate dynamism, so that any farsighted entrepreneur must look for it. This means watching economic developments very closely. Modern communications very quickly spread the word about new openings, and the strategic windows are not open for long. Some company or other will seize an opportunity as soon as it is barely discernible and occupy the strategic position, whereupon the window closes for firms coming in later. A dynamic management team must therefore aim to exploit new value potential as quickly as possible and occupy the strategic positions, for a number of reasons.[4]

Study of the PIMS database[5] shows that the pioneers, which enter the market and occupy the relevant positions first, achieve a higher return on investment than the companies which follow their lead.[6] We can infer that the rules governing entry into the market apply broadly speaking to all value potential. Hanson, for instance, was the first firm back in the 1960s to start taking over and restructuring 'undermanaged companies'. Firms which develop value potential early on will also reap the benefits of the learning curve, learning more quickly than other companies how to make the most of the potential. Simon's view on the psychological significance of early entry and the rapid occupation of strategic positions is interesting, too: 'We see it as most important from the competitive standpoint that the pioneer occupies a blank space on the cognitive map of the consumer, a chance that no one else has – or, as Ries and Trout express it: "The easy way to get into a person's mind is to be first".'[7] Once again what goes for market potential also goes for all value potential. Electrolux soon made a name for itself in the white goods sector, as other companies noticed how it was increasingly taking over and restructuring firms. As a result practically everyone wanting to sell a white goods company approached Electrolux first.

Value potential is often very short-lived, another reason to accelerate business procedures. Now that health authorities have such stringent standards, the registration of drugs can take so long that patent protection expires only a few years after the product arrives on the market. Hence the need to speed up registration by applying for it at the same time in different countries, rather than sequentially.

Introduction into the market, though, is the time when speed really counts. In 1983 Sarna AG began to develop a concept for roof gardens. It fitted in perfectly with current trends and restored the tarnished image of the flat roof. The construction market, however, takes a while to accept innovations, so to save time the product was presented at trade fairs before it was ready to go into production. Sarna was able to test the mood of the market and establish requirements in detail before investing heavily in special facilities.

Acceleration may also be called for on grounds of cost. When Nokia took over the Swedish television manufacturer, Luxor, it had to restructure it very fast because it was operating at a loss. Every day without change added to the damage to the company's accounts. In opening its stores so quickly, Metro is largely concerned to cover its capital investment in land and buildings as soon as possible.

How do dynamic companies save time and speed themselves up?

The corporate concept can lay a good foundation for acceleration. Provided it is based on a consensus among the key executives and defines clear priorities, it can save a great deal of time. Everyone knows which way the company is going. It can concentrate immediately on strategically important activities, rejecting any which fall outside the concept before any time is wasted on them.

A clear concept allows you, for example, to apply the 80/20 rule: 80 per cent of a result is decided by 20 per cent of the factors. (For example: 20 per cent of the customers provide 80 per cent of turnover: 20 per cent of the products raise 80 per cent of turnover, etc.) Using this concept directs the company towards those 20 per cent of activities which achieve a relatively great effect, ie great leverage, with relatively little input – obviously the activities which develop attractive value potential. The other 80 per cent, which yield much less, can be neglected, saving considerable time which can then be used on the key activities.

Processes can be speeded up by increasing the input of resources. In the 1970s, for example, one company going through the critical turnaround phase hired a whole team of management consultants to help operational management implement the necessary changes as quickly as possible. In turnaround situations particularly a massive input of resources can contribute substantially to rapid improvement.

Time can also be saved by finding creative ways of doing things faster. Glaxo's co-marketing idea, which we have already mentioned, was certainly innovative and creative: until the late 1970s it was practically unthinkable that a pharmaceutical concern should use a rival's marketing organization to develop a market faster. Glaxo broke out of the rut and thus achieved the quickest and most successful product introduction in pharmaceutical history. Of course innovations of this kind are very soon imitated. Within a few years the idea of co-marketing had been adopted by various well-known competitors such as Merck & Co., Squibb, Rhone Poulenc, Upjohn and others.[8]

Creative innovations can speed up processes in all functions. For instance, marketing, production and development can all be involved at the same time in production development, right from the start.

Modern information technology has revolutionized whole sectors such as commodity trading. Transactions that just a few years ago used to take hours or days can now be carried out in fractions of a second. As information technology progresses there will be even more spectacular time savings in future, offering great opportunities to those firms which are ready to take them.

Cooperative ventures and alliances can also help acceleration. Glaxo's co-marketing is a step in this direction, and in many sectors cooperation, often with erstwhile bitter rivals, has become the order of the day. We have only to think of the close cooperative network of motor manufacturers spanning the continents. In the electronics sector, too, joint ventures which would have been unthinkable a few years ago are now a matter of course. Philips and Siemens are developing 64-megabit chips together. Siemens and IBM are collaborating on the UNIX operating system. The point of this cooperation is ultimately to concentrate resources synergically and thus allow business processes to keep pace with the extremely dynamic development of the market and the business environment. The time factor is forcing companies to make their boundaries less rigid.

We have already touched on two other possible ways of working quickly: decentralization and the formation of autonomous subsystems, and a dynamically oriented corporate culture. Both can contribute equally to the acceleration of business procedures.[9]

Guidelines for management

Time management

The entrepreneurial manager organizes his or her working time in such a way that a large part of it is spent on expansionary activities. They concentrate on attractive value potential and on multiplying the activities that relate to it.

Timing

Dynamic managers are well aware that timing is crucial, and base theirs on the analysis of information, their personal experience and not least intuition.

Acceleration

The dynamic company hums with energy, momentum and a thirst for action. Skilfully conceived, creative measures are introduced and processes are reorganized from the ground up in order to save time. More autonomous teams are used.

Notes

1   I have already made these points in one of my earlier books; see Pümpin, 1989.
2   See also Abell, 1978, pp. 21–6.
3   See Leysen, 1988, p. 103.
4   See also Simon, 1988, pp. 14ff.
5   Buzzell and Gale's periodic PIMS studies (Profit Impact of Market Strategy) draw on a database with information on about 3,000 strategic business units in Europe and America to analyse the effects of different variables (market share, growth, R & D projects, quality standards, etc,.) on the ROI, ROS, etc. See Buzzell and Gale, 1987.
6   See Clifford and Cavanagh, 1986.
7   Simon, op. cit., p. 21; he quotes from Ries and Trout, 1986, p. 19.
8   Simon, op. cit., p.18.
9   See also Simon, op. cit., pp. 10ff.

Chapter 9

Risk: the price of dynamism

The risks of dynamic development

Increasing the benefits for stakeholders in a relatively short time entails a substantial increase in the number of business transactions or in the volume of business. Expansion of this kind is bound to involve risks.

The firms we considered for this project are positive examples: they have reached their goals. It was not the intention of this book to analyse companies whose planned dynamic expansion had failed, although it might well be worth investigating the causes and implications of such failures.[1]

Why, then, is dynamic corporate development such a risky business? The dynamic company has to develop attractive value potential, potential which is always changing, always moving on. Moving objects are by nature less stable than static ones and can more easily be overturned. Therein lies one of the most important causes of risk.

Sooner or later the dynamic company will have to harness new value potential, which is risky simply because it is an unknown quantity. The risks can occur in any area of business, as we are about to see.

Where to look out for risks

Dynamic companies will face risks in areas such as:

* *Innovation*, if the company's new product is not in harmony with the

targeted value potential. One example is quadrophony, which made considerable losses when it was launched in the 1970s at great expense, but failed to make an impact and had to be taken off the market.

- *Turnover,* when the potential market or other value potential turns out to be less fertile than expected. This can arise either because the need for the product is relatively low, or, more often, because changes in the environment and in the marketplace reduce demand. For instance, when new laws severely restricted the use of asbestos because of the danger to health, manufacturers of asbestos products found their turnover collapsing. There are risks for restructurers in the restrictions on company takeovers which some governments are projecting.
- *Competition:* when several competitors target the same value potential at the same time, the benefit each can reap will be lower than expected, and some may even make a loss. In 1988 the market for personal computers in Europe was very attractive and expanding strongly, but as PC dealers fought over market share the margins collapsed and some firms went to the wall. The same can happen with other value potential: intensive competition in company acquisitions has lifted prices to a point at which the benefits of mergers are beginning to seem dubious.
- *Finance:* companies sometimes expand so fast that they cannot finance the growth. In particular they often have insufficient resources to cover current assets, especially debtors and stocks.
- *Costs:* expansion strategies often assume that costs will be reduced by the learning curve as volume increases. Similarly, company takeovers may be based on the assumption that unit costs can be cut by merging activities. Although this works in theory and often in practice, sometimes the costs fail to decrease.
- *Organization:* takeovers can be so disturbing that all the projected advantages are wiped out. A mismatch of corporate cultures can lead to 'culture shock', or the leadership potential may be inadequate. As a result the whole system gets out of control and collapses.

This short overview is intended simply to highlight the greatest risks. There are many others: purchasing risks (sources of supply dry up), information risk (the information technology cannot keep pace with the expansion and breaks down), union risk (the trade unions unexpectedly interfere), assessment risk in company takeovers and so on. The real danger lies in the unexpected risks which the company overlooks, as it takes steps to limit or avoid the obvious ones.

Since dynamic companies run great risks, they have to have a clear risk policy incorporating certain principles.

Risk principles

It is, of course, up to every company to set out and implement its own independent risk policy. Companies which succeed in the long term, however, do tend to adhere to a number of concrete principles.

Measured expansion

Now and again there are isolated firms which expand unimaginably fast. Take the computer firm Sun Microsystems (as well as the equally explosive Compaq), which for the years 1983 to 1987 showed an average growth in turnover of 127 per cent. Expansion of this kind is inherently rare. There is a great danger that the necessary resources will be in short supply and that sooner or later difficulties will cause a setback or even total collapse. The development of Commodore and Atari has shown this pattern.

Many of the companies we looked at were not aiming at expansion above all, but tried to expand in a steady, sustainable way. Thus, for example, for years American Express has aimed for and achieved a growth rate of between 15 and 20 per cent. Such growth allows the company to develop harmoniously and manage its expansion as well as possible.

Cash-generating value potential

There is a strong link between growth and value potential which generates cash. Static firms are all too often satisfied with tiny margins. They are happy to be achieving any turnover at all, or to be maintaining market share, and not making a loss. In other cases projects are backed by a financial policy which makes profit on paper (say, by depreciation accounting) but is actually a cash drain over the years.

Net cash flow and return on capital employed are the key figures for dynamic companies, which accordingly only develop potential which will guarantee a positive cash flow and reasonable interest on capital employed, before too long.

Defining an emphasis

The issue of diversity is often raised. Many managers hold the view that risks are reduced by involvement in as many different activities as possible, so that setbacks in one part of a conglomerate can be offset by positive developments in another. This is not always true, however; according to research the shares of many conglomerates perform below the stock market indices in the long term,[2] which indicates that this policy tends to be inefficient. In other words, too wide a diversity is very risky as far as financial results are concerned.

In fact, concentrating on quite a narrow field of activity can carry less risk than a diverse programme. For example, the Hilti company, which makes fastening systems for the building trade, was actually able to increase its market share during a recession in the construction market. Its competitors with interests in other markets were retreating into areas where there was less pressure, but Hilti was forced to assert itself and the extra effort paid off. In practically all its branches it was able to build up a strong market position, thus considerably reducing risks.

This example is only meant to show the dangers of too wide a diversification and the advantages of concentrating energies. In many cases it is wise to aim for a reasonable distribution of risks, but not at the expense of a harmonious corporate concept. The emphasis of the company should be clearly defined.

Matching the end to the means

Far too many firms have expanded strongly in a favourable economic situation, stretching their financial and human resources. When a recession unexpectedly arrives there is a liquidity crisis or insufficiently experienced management to bring the setbacks under control. Ski manufacturer Howard Head had this unpleasant experience in 1970. Aggressive expansion in the second half of the 1960s had made great demands on his own resources, especially cash. In the winter of 1969/70 there was very little snow, so not many skis were sold and he was left with large stocks. The resulting cash crisis obliged him to sell the company.

Rhythmic expansion

Another way to restrict the level of risks is to establish a rhythm whereby periods of consolidation are built in after periods of expansion. At Bertelsmann, for instance, they feel it is very important to have a consolidation phase after every major acquisition in order to integrate the firm they have just taken over, and especially to build up a relationship of constructive cooperation with the managers of the new member of the group.

Risk containment

Dynamic firms deliberately find ways of limiting risks, taking all kinds of precautions. Hanson lays great weight on carefully calculating the 'downside risk' of every acquisition – the expected financial loss in the worst possible case. Only when the downside risk falls within acceptable limits does the acquisition go ahead.

Adequate reserves

Finally, every dynamic company knows that it can never rule out risks altogether. A sufficient strategic reserve must therefore always be available.

This is mostly a question of making sure that enough financial assets are available in an emergency. But management resources should not be underestimated. A number of companies have got into trouble because of insufficient management capacity.

The risks of the free market economy

We live in a turbulent world, where a company can only survive in the long term by adapting to change. Without dynamics companies become rigid and lose their ability to adapt. The economic press reports dozens of such cases. The future looks equally challenging, as economic integration proceeds both in Europe and overseas and more rapid technological advances and social, legal and political changes are in the pipeline. Static firms run the risk of being caught out sooner or later and facing takeover, liquidation or bankruptcy.

In such an environment the company must try to find and develop new value potential, a risky business.

Today's company, then, lives in permanent conflict. If it does not adapt there is the danger that changes will bring its profits crashing down. On the other hand adapting is dangerous as well. The dynamic company recognizes the dilemma. It knows that any economic activity carries risks and that failure to adapt is often riskier than change oriented to the future. With this in mind it makes a firm decision to take on the risks associated with expansion, but to keep them under control through a sensible risk policy.

Guidelines for management

Risk and dynamics go together

The dynamic manager knows that risk and enterprise are inseparable, and is prepared to take risks.

Risk principles

The dynamic manager calculates the risks precisely and pursues a clearly
defined risk policy built on solid principles.

Notes

1   A very valuable examination of this subject was undertaken by John
    Argenti. See Argenti, 1976.
2   See eg Porter, 1987.

Epilogue

Corporate dynamism and management theory

Management theories as blanket solutions

Business management theory has, broadly speaking, changed its emphasis in every decade since the Second World War. The prevailing economic, technological, ecological, demographic and social conditions have dictated how problems are formulated and consequently the kind of solutions that are offered.

Immediately after the Second World War the greatest challenge was to find the money for reconstruction. Finance and cost management were the central issues, as well as technical problems related to the construction of production plant.

By the 1960s the picture had changed. The customer had started to discriminate, and was no longer prepared to buy everything that was produced. The focus moved to marketing. Farsighted companies discovered that they needed to be stronger, and some medium-sized and larger companies introduced divisional organization. Improving the company in general became much more important, though the approach in those days was rather more bureaucratic than today.[1]

In the 1970s markets were becoming glutted, and the oil crisis churned up the economic waters. Competitive strategies came to the fore, supposedly helping companies to assert themselves over the competition. Even then, however, perceptive managers saw that a more comprehensive solution was needed to solve the problems of the future, and many adopted the systems approach.

But as we entered the 1980s the results of analytical strategies were often disappointing. Head offices, overburdened with strategic staff and bureaucracy, had lost touch with the front line. Then the USA, till then the leading economic nation, found itself contending with serious economic problems. It was time to change the parameters. Strategy was replaced by excellence. More copies of *In Search of Excellence* were printed than of any other non-fiction book. However, this management approach has its limits, too, and many of the 'excellent' companies quoted by Peters and Waterman are now in unexpected difficulties.

Corporate dynamism: the solution for the 1990s

The dynamic principles conceived here fit logically into this historical context. Dynamism can be seen as the answer to the problems of the late twentieth-century post-industrial society. In today's volatile environment the long-term survivors are those companies which are dynamic enough to adapt quickly to new developments, seize the opportunities and deflect the dangers.

The investigation of dynamic companies on which this book is based shows that some are using concepts which conflict with the familiar approaches of competitive strategy and excellence. Most of all they demonstrate that dynamics can be generated by harnessing not only market potential but all kinds of other potential as well, such as financial potential, acquisition potential, balance sheet potential, organizational potential, and so on – summed up by the new term 'value potential'. This more flexible outlook is gaining significance as sales markets in the post-industrial economies are rapidly reaching saturation, and new value potential has to be developed.

Dynamic companies are also evolving a new understanding of the company.

- Survival is no longer the ultimate goal, as classic management theory has it. This does not mean that companies should take on the character of projects and be dissolved as soon as the project is finished, but that there is considerable room for manoeuvre in the area of company takeovers, as recent developments have shown.
- Greater structural flexibility is the order of the day. The company's structures should be kept under review and flexibly reorganized to suit current requirements. This may mean separating out some parts of the company, perhaps disposing of them or even closing them

down, or new units may have to be incorporated.

- Thirdly, the boundaries of the company are becoming in many ways more fluid. Joint ventures, minority stakes, cooperation and innovative forms of collaboration such as networks are on the increase. It is also becoming harder to distinguish the functional boundaries of the company. Kohlberg, Kravis, Roberts (KKR), the leveraged buyout company, can be looked at in two different ways. It sees itself as a small finance 'boutique' with about twenty employees. *Fortune* magazine, on the other hand, places KKR right behind IBM as the fifth largest US concern, including in its portfolio such companies as RJR–Nabisco (around $16,000m. turnover), Beatrice Companies (around $9,000m.), Owens Illinois ($3,700m.). KKR does not publish any consolidated accounts, but its total turnover including RJR in 1988 was estimated to be about $54,000m.[2] *Fortune*'s point of view is supported by the fact that KKR exercises full control over all the firms it acquires. Incidentally: these comments are not intended as a justification of the distinctly problematical financial transactions of a company such as KKR, but simply to point out what may be a growing difficulty in post-industrial societies.

  Hanson plc is in a similar situation. It does publish a consolidated business report, revealing in 1988 a turnover of £7,369m. and a personnel of over 105,000. Yet Martin G. Taylor, its Vice Chairman, told me that Hanson could just as well be described as a smallish consultancy firm, with barely fifty professionals, specializing in restructuring and efficient management. The only difference from other firms of consultants would be that Hanson buys the companies it is to 'advise' and thus ensures that its recommendations are implemented. Many an experienced consultant would acknowledge the wisdom of this idea!

These and other examples point to a new entrepreneurial concept: the 'fluid company'. Such a company has a flexible structure, and no longer sees itself and its component parts as given quantities. Its aim is to generate benefits for its stakeholders, who are moving into the spotlight of this new concept.

This shift in priorities has far-reaching implications. If the company's survival is only justified as long as it is generating benefits for its stakeholders, then as soon as there is doubt about whether benefits are being generated the point of the company's continued existence is put in question. This may be an uncomfortable thesis at first glance. But we accept that all living systems have a life cycle marked off at the end by death. Why should the same not be true of companies? Or there is the ecological viewpoint, which calls for more goods to be recycled. Hans A.

Wüthrich has suggested that the recycling idea should be applied to companies as well. Skilful recycling could give a new lease of life to companies in decline.

The stakeholder view has other implications too. It gives more weight to those stakeholders who actually contribute to the generation of value – nowadays increasingly the bearers of expertise and those who play an active role in the company. There are signs that these stakeholders are becoming more powerful: management buyouts and the Employee Stock Ownership Plan (ESOP), under which the company is controlled not just by the management but by the whole workforce. Leveraged buyouts can also be explained by this point of view, since in many cases the aim is to increase the profits not only of shareholders but also of investment fund owners.

This perspective makes sense of the accumulation of corporate transactions in the late twentieth century. New economic pioneers are trying to break up the corporate and economic structures which arose after the Second World War and put into practice the economic concepts which best fit with the current of the times.

The dynamic principle as corporate concept

In recent times there have been a number of important new management approaches. Rappaport's 'shareholder value approach' is related to the stakeholder approach insofar as it moves one particular interest group – the shareholders – into the spotlight.[3] Porter's competitive strategy approach and the excellence approach of Peters and Waterman should also be mentioned.

In this book I have tried to integrate the various management approaches. While repeatedly stressing the importance of creating benefits for all stakeholders, I have also emphasized that shareholder profit must not be neglected. Of course competitive strategy and excellence have an important part to play within the framework of corporate dynamism.

I should like to make it clear at this point that these latter two approaches especially will continue to be extremely important. In most firms success will be measured by performance in the marketplace, and here competitive superiority and excellence play a fundamental role. The dynamic approach, however, shows that there is other potential than market potential and that the dynamic company may find it better to tackle these other types of potential. It also stipulates that tasks should be approached unconventionally and without the cumbersome restrictions of past history. A wider view must be taken, and all value potential should be considered.

The dynamic approach is thus an attempt to develop a corporate concept. The corporate concept, like Porter's corporate strategy, contrasts with competitive strategy:

- Competitive strategy is mainly directed to achieving competitive advantage in the marketplace.
- Corporate strategy is directed mainly to generating benefits for the stakeholders by exploiting value potential.

Both are long-term strategies, while the dynamic approach is more flexible about time. In harnessing value potential to energize the company, the overriding criterion is stakeholder value, rather than timespan. Multiplying the development of value potential in the short and medium term can also generate dynamics and is therefore worthwhile.

The dynamic approach can hence be seen as (Porterian) corporate strategy extended to include greater flexibility, in comparison with the rather limited competitive strategy.

It might be interesting to subdivide corporate dynamism into the classic categories of strategy, planning, organization and so on, but that would be to relapse into the formal patterns of thought which I have attempted to break out of with the introduction of value potential and multiplication. The aim of this book is to make management less formal and more action-oriented.

All in all, I hope that the entrepreneurial solutions suggested by my dynamic approach will be of growing significance in the years to come. I have tried to give the open-minded, enterprising manager some practical impulses to shape the future of his company.

Twelve theses on corporate dynamism

The most important points of the book are summarized in these twelve theses. Two things should be borne in mind while reading them:

- Following the majority of the twelve theses is enough to generate dynamics. Only very rarely does a company practise all twelve at once.
- For the sake of clarity I have oversimplified the twelve theses and painted a stark contrast between dynamic and static behaviour.

Thesis 1
Dynamic companies develop attractive value potential

Developing attractive value potential is the nub of corporate dynamism. Value potential is attractive if developing it will generate significant value for the company's stakeholders.

Dynamic companies consistently concentrate on attractive value potential.

Static companies concern themselves with value potential which is losing its attraction, and try frantically to squeeze the last drops from it. Their ability to give value to their stakeholders is therefore limited.

Thesis 2
Dynamic companies are broad-minded and creative in their search for attractive value potential

Dynamic companies have seen that the markets in post-industrial societies are reaching saturation, so that market potential is losing its attraction. They therefore take an unconventional and creative approach to value potential, looking for it everywhere, both inside and outside the company.

Static companies stay with the status quo and hence often with unattractive value potential. They are too dogmatic to consider new value potential.

Thesis 3
Dynamic companies multiply business activities

As soon as their output has noticeable advantages over the alternatives, dynamic companies steadily multiply the activities which harness the value potential.

Static companies do not multiply, preferring to tie up their resources in unnecessarily perfecting their output.

Thesis 4
Dynamic companies multiply sophisticated processes and systems

The output of dynamic companies is highly developed and hard to copy. They multiply complex processes and deliberately exploit every possibility of multiplying systems.

Static companies are content to make and sell products in the traditional way.

Thesis 5
Dynamic companies achieve leverage

With attractive value potential, demand for the company's valuable output will increase, creating its own momentum. Lower costs and other advantages follow from multiplication, adding to the initial momentum and creating a powerful lever effect.

Static companies are oblivious to the benefits of leverage and make no attempt to achieve it.

Thesis 6
Dynamic companies increase the benefits for their stakeholders several times over

Dynamic companies generate benefits for all their stakeholders. They promote the welfare of everyone with an interest in the company, a valuable and ethically sound purpose.

Static companies focus on the benefits of individual interest groups – usually the holders of power. They neglect or even wholly ignore other stakeholders.

Thesis 7
Dynamic companies have one or more growth promoters to sustain the dynamic forces

One or more energetic growth promoters within the dynamic company instigate the multiplicative development of value potential and keep it going. They are highly ambitious and set above-average goals for themselves and the company.

Static companies are run by bureaucrats and technocrats who see it as their task to preserve the status quo. The balance of power excludes growth promoters. The chief objectives of top management are to hold on to power and protect their assets.

Thesis 8
Dynamic companies develop and build a cohesive corporate concept

The central plank of the dynamic company is its harmonious and cohesive corporate concept, which provides the best framework within which to exploit value potential.

Static companies are mechanically managed, with the emphasis on the systematic organization of existing activities.

Thesis 9
Dynamic companies create flexible, liberating structures

The constitution of dynamic companies facilitates their flexible development and allows structures which are fair to people and equally fair to the demands of a turbulent business world. Their chief characteristics are autonomous units and flat organizational structures.

Static companies use a mountain of unnecessary documents to regulate jobs, authority and responsibility. They use bureaucracy to shield them from the dangers of the turbulent environment and do not see the opportunities presented by change.

Thesis 10
Dynamic companies are people-oriented

Dynamic companies motivate their employees in every possible way. Man-management is a crucial element in dynamic development. The culture is oriented to expansion, speed, productivity and risk-taking.

The management of static companies is content to pay lip service to motivation. What culture they have is dominated by bureaucracy and cost awareness. They neglect the time factor.

Thesis 11
Dynamic companies make best use of the resource of time

Dynamic companies know how to exploit that critical resource, time, to best effect. Major business activities are carefully timed and tasks are carried out quickly. The top executives allocate most of their own time to expansive tasks.

In static companies the emphasis is on being busy, rather than on efficiency and productivity. Top executives devote their time to maintaining the status quo or furthering their personal interests.

Thesis 12
Dynamic companies pursue a risk policy built on clearly defined principles

Dynamic companies overcome risks by adhering to a number of concrete principles. They are aware that every entrepreneurial activity entails risks, and that failure to act can often prove more dangerous still, and are therefore prepared to take calculated risks.

Static companies are afraid of risks, and if in doubt avoid taking action.

Notes

1   See Höhn, 1966.
2   See Loomis, 1988, pp. 53 ff.
3   See Rappaport, 1986.

Case studies

Five dynamic companies

Bertelsmann

By 1946 the German 'Christian publishing house of Carl Bertelsmann' was 111 years old and the life's work of four generations of Bertelsmanns and Mohns. It was also in ruins, reduced by the Second World War to a heap of rubble.

Since its foundation Bertelsmann had been a middle-ranking company, but now its development literally exploded. A turnover of 1m. DM in 1948 had become 10,500m. DM by 1988. The average rate of growth in the 1950s was 42 per cent, in the 1960s 15 per cent, in the 1970s 21 per cent, and since 1980 it has been 10 per cent (ie an extra 1,000m. DM turnover a year!) The number of employees rose from about 200 to 42,000.

How did this development come about?

Value potential

Reinhard Mohn, head of the firm since the end of the war, focused on three kinds of value potential:

Market potential

Mohn saw tremendous value potential in the growing demand for books. After the nineteenth century the split in society between the 'educated' and the 'uneducated' had begun to disappear, and Bertelsmann had already started to sell sophisticated literature to a much wider public after the First World War.

Mohn went further in this direction. Bertelsmann made a name for its popular editions of literature as well as general interest books, encyclopedias and other reference books.

The real growth spurt, however, came from the idea of the 'reading circle', the book club. For the first time Bertelsmann brought books to a broad stratum of society which had previously been afraid to buy them. Only four years after its foundation on 1 June 1950 the 'reading circle' had one million members, and three years later two million.[1] Today it has 22 million members all over the world. In the wake of the book club other areas such as the technical businesses and publishing houses were able to grow, too.

In the 1960s, 1970s and 1980s new market potential was consistently developed: records, magazines, paperbacks and audiovisual material, not only in West Germany but worldwide.

Human potential

The attractive market potential of the media has been exploited by a large number of other competitors, so it cannot on its own account for Mohn's success. Mohn's unique achievement is that he, far ahead of his time, recognized the crucial importance of human potential. Chief executive Marc Wössner said: 'The mainly fallow creative resources of a large number of workers represent real potential which, if successfully mobilized, will clinch competitive advantage. The sustained mobilization of these resources seems to us to be attainable only by motivation and the identification of the individual with his job.'

Mohn's efforts to develop human potential were revolutionary. He strove for a corporate constitution which gave employees great freedom and hence enabled creative development. His master stroke was the participation model. At Bertelsmann employee participation was already widespread in the 1950s. High identification and motivation resulted, and Bertelsmann had a strong image in the labour market. Thanks to its outstanding reputation as an innovative employer, many highly qualified executives and employees applied to the company, and this human potential significantly strengthened its productivity. No less important, however, joint participation in the company supplied the financial resources urgently needed for expansion.

Technology

The thrust of technology in the media after the Second World War presented a third kind of value potential. Bertelsmann was able to turn the dramatic developments in electronics to its advantage. The unstoppable technological progress in communications promises yet more exciting opportunities.

Parallel development of value potential

Bertelsmann's example demonstrates the tremendous dynamism which can be developed by exploiting several kinds of value potential simultaneously and synergically. Bertelsmann did not restrict itself to market potential, but by combining value potential became much more dynamic than any of its competitors.

Multiplication

Another factor in Bertelsmann's success was the extremely consistent multiplication of its business activities at various levels:

Internationalization

Firstly Bertelsmann made its original business international, transferring the book club concept, for instance, to countries such as France and Spain. Its sales expertise, with certain modifications, worked well in other countries. France now has the largest book club in the world, with about 5 million members. The Spanish club is a cultural success as well as a commercial one, since it has also become an unprecedented writers' forum.

Product launching

Bertelsmann successfully transferred its expertise in magazines to marketing organizations in Spain, France, England and the USA. Its market position in these countries was greatly reinforced by the introduction of existing magazines from other markets – multiplying product launches.

'Special interest magazines'

In West Germany Bertelsmann pioneered special interest magazines, bringing out in rapid succession titles on sports, nature and food, multiplying the expertise it acquired in the field.

Growth promoter

Reinhard Mohn was an outstanding promoter of dynamism. It was his conviction and vision that helped to develop the publishing house into the media giant we see today. Above all he discovered and developed considerable market, human and technological potential.

His dynamic style was that of an accelerator:

- The value potential was all freely available. It only needed to be exploited, quickly, synergically and multiplicatively.
- Mohn, as chief executive, had a direct influence on the running of the business.
- He set ambitious goals.
- He sought out young managers and gave them the freedom they needed.
- He used innovative means of motivation.

Corporate concept

We have seen that Bertelsmann consistently applied the dynamic principle of a dynamic growth promoter identifying value potential in several areas and developing it in a multiplicative way. Its corporate concept, according to Marc Wössner, has been the central element in its dynamic development.

Under the headings

- The aims of the company
- Responsibility to society
- Entrepreneurial leadership and organization
- Partnership in the company

the corporate concept formally sets out and explains the orientation of the company. Its strategic and motivational power make it a source of corporate dynamics and helps to distinguish Bertelsmann from other media concerns.

The whole corporate concept is based on the idea that 'Communication is our job'. This theme is an expression of the entrepreneur's vision of making a contribution to society. It is made concrete in a few, telling, corporate objectives which combine with it to form a harmonious whole, a solid foundation for dynamic corporate development. Statements such as the following create the basis for a clear strategic direction:

We are:
concentrating on the media
internationally active
decentralized
pluralistic in our projects
employee-oriented

committed to social policy
culturally oriented.

They are also the foundation stones of motivation and give a sense of purpose in a world which is becoming ever more difficult to comprehend.

Structures

Bertelsmann solved the problem of increasing size by the most extensive decentralization. The central board 'leads from the centre' and lays down the basis for the corporate policy and guidelines for operational management, as well as steering corporate development. The operational responsibility for each individual business, however, remains entirely with the head of that business.

Mohn says of this: 'With this decentralization we have created entrepreneurial freedom for those responsible at the head of the individual profit centres, releasing the power of creative and entrepreneurially-minded people which is essential for the company's continued development and ability to compete.'[2] Or Dr Wössner, elsewhere: 'The principle of delegation has brought a driving force into the company; the profit centres, which operate independently in the marketplace, have always been the engines and supports of the dynamic development of our house.'[3]

Wherever possible Bertelsmann has tried to attract younger managers to head the profit centres. Offering responsibility to younger people has enabled the company to acquire some highly qualified executives.

Man-management

We saw the variety of Bertelsmann's social efforts in the paragraph headed 'Human potential', above, and here we shall summarize only the most important motivating measures:

1 Wide-ranging delegation of duties and responsibility
2 Unconventional opportunities to participate in decisions
3 Participation in profits and extensive financial and non-financial incentives
4 Cultivation of a feeling of belonging to the foremost and most progressive media company.

Bertelsmann's corporate culture is an important instrument in encouraging dynamism amongst the personnel.

Time

Bertelsmann's view of time is interesting. Newly identified value potential is developed extremely rapidly. With the book club, for instance, the strategic positions had to be occupied as fast as possible, and newly acquired companies are very quickly integrated. When Doubleday was taken over recently, it was broken up within six months and allocated to the various divisions of Bertelsmann. Bertelsmann can be said, therefore, to act very quickly.

But significant steps in expansion are timed in rhythmic phases: a major acquisition is always followed by a period of consolidation. Important expansions are always very carefully prepared, as well. Plenty of time is spent on analysis and on building up the necessary management potential.

Risk

Bertelsmann cuts down the risks in various ways. We can briefly mention three. Firstly it only develops value potential for which it has the necessary expertise. Secondly, it tackles value potential step by step. For instance, small projects are used when entering a new market in order to gain some familiarity with the culture and idiosyncracies of the country. Thirdly, experienced executives are placed alongside new managers, spreading the culture and thus contributing to the containment of risks.

Cartier

Three generations created the renown of the French house of Cartier as the world's best-known jewellers. Louis François, who founded the company in 1847, was presented at court by Princesse Mathilde, a cousin of Napoleon II, and celebrated his first successes with his valuable collection. His son Albert set up the present family firm at Rue de la Paix 13, which was taken over in 1900 by the founder's grandson, Louis, at the same time as his brothers, Jacques and Pierre, were opening branches in London and New York.

Louis's tasteful inventions strengthened the fame of Cartier. His timeless designs for jewellery, clocks and accessories are recorded in the 'sketchbook' – the treasure chest which underlies the success of the present-day firm of Cartier. King Edward VII, when Prince of Wales, called him the 'jeweller of kings and the king of jewellers'. He had ready access to fifteen royal houses as purveyor to the court. Cartier was the ultimate jeweller.

After Louis's death in 1942 the Cartier Group lived on its past. The three branches each went their own way.

In 1969 Cartier began to develop into a group which was active worldwide. The shops in Paris, London and New York were financially merged and put under the same management. The industrialist, Robert Hocq, one of the leading manufacturers of luxury cigarette lighters, was licensed to use and commercialize the Cartier brand name. When Cartier Paris was taken over by an international group of investors in 1972, Hocq was given the leadership of the Group.

Hocq appointed Alain-Dominique Perrin, then only 26 years old, to sell the 'Briquet', the oval Cartier lighter. Together they turned the jeweller's into one of the foremost luxury concerns in the world for jewellery and related products. Its success is astonishing: Cartier's annual growth is 20–25 per cent. In 1970 its turnover was $8.3m., in 1988 $710m.

Value potential

Image potential

Cartier was altogether one of the most famous names in jewellery. It was associated with an image of excellence. Hocq and Perrin recognized the tremendous power which lay in the image and hence the name of Cartier, and set themselves the goal of building Cartier up from a jeweller to a luxury brand.

They exploited the image potential of the time-honoured house of Cartier by the familiar traditional methods of marketing the brand and taking good care of it. The brand image was not at any cost to be damaged. First distribution had to be controlled by a coherent course of action:

*   The first step was to bring the three houses in Paris, London and New York back under common management and to make the range uniform.
*   Secondly, Hocq and Perrin created 'Les Must de Cartier' and succeeded in persuading their public that though, like all luxuries, they were not actually necessary, one simply 'must' have them. All of 'les Must' are taken from designs in Louis Cartier's sketchbook. Today the range embraces jewellery, clocks, perfumes, lighters, writing implements, spectacles, leatherware, scarves and table settings. The innovation consisted not so much in the creation of new products as in the new way they were marketed.
*   Thirdly, every detail of their marketing is precise, a concept Cartier sees as its own invention. The greatest attention is paid to the distribution policy. Only the boutiques sell the jewellery, and they also stock the entire Must range. The concessionaires sell whichever Musts fit in with their own business, so lighters are sold by

tobacconists, spectacles by opticians, perfumes in perfumeries and so on.

- In addition Cartier controls prices very vigilantly: its dealers are allowed, at least in the beginning, a very generous profit margin, but the retail sales prices are laid down by the concern, so that a customer pays the same for a Must in Rio de Janeiro as in London or Paris. Discounts to customers are not allowed. The company had a hard fight to achieve this, but it protected the value of the brand. For the same reason Cartier commissions all its own goods and gives no production licences.

Cartier is not content with simply exploiting image potential: it also takes trouble to enhance it. For some time the company has sponsored the exclusive sport of polo. Sport sponsorship is one of the best known marketing methods, but Cartier has elevated it to an art. It has also come up with a new kind of sponsorship: the patronage of art. Cartier presented its thoughts on a new generation of patrons of the arts in a memorandum to the French Minister of Culture. In Jouy-en-Josas, near Paris, the company created the 'Fondation Cartier pour l'art contemporain', a fifteen-hectare exhibition area showing the work of over 170 contemporary artists. It also provides artists with space and financial support for their work. This patronage has a positive effect on Cartier's image, especially amongst the young people who are the potential customers of the future. Its involvement with modern art has also found favour with the press, who have previously been all too happy to attack Cartier.

Market potential

Hocq and Perrin were the first to recognize that luxury articles would represent some of the greatest value potential before the end of the century. It was estimated in 1969 that there were 6,000 good jewellers in the world, but unlike in other sectors there were no real brand names. Meanwhile the industrialized world has experienced an unprecedented boom since the Second World War. Many fortunes have been made, and it is no longer only the aristocracy and landed gentry who can afford jewellery and other luxury items.

Les Must de Cartier are also genuine investments. Their timeless design and high-quality materials make them valuable heirlooms. Cartier refuses to make Musts which depend on fashion, or which have little creative merit. The 'Santos' clock today, for example, is exactly the same as the model designed by Louis Cartier in 1907. Cartier would never sell ties or other fashion-dependent products. Cigarettes are an exception to the rule, attributable to Cartier's connection with the Rothmans group.

Multiplication

Perrin himself took a case of sample lighters to tobacconists throughout Europe and thus found his first concessionaires. The lighter was a hit. Once the three original shops had been reunited under one management, Perrin instituted a sharply defined distribution policy of system multiplication – branches and shops – and process multiplication – negotiation of contracts with concessionaires. Worldwide Cartier now has 31 wholly-owned branches, and 127 franchised shops in which the firm has majority control. Seven thousand dealers hold concessions to handle Cartier products.

But Cartier even controls its growth: its existing production capacity would be enough for double the turnover. However, at Cartier they are aware that for healthy growth the organization, communications, logistics and especially the personnel capacity have to keep pace with the development of the firm. The profits from Cartier's growth allow the company's strategy to be implemented and consolidate the brand profile. The current average growth rate is 20–25 per cent. 'Less growth would be complacent, more growth too risky.'

Cartier also multiplies its expertise in the management of branded goods, and is associated with such brands as Yves Saint Laurent, Ferrari and John Sterling. The acquisition of Piaget and of Baume & Mercier gave Cartier the lead in the luxury market, with a total market share of 40 per cent. It claims to be first in jewellery, second in lighters and luxury writing wares and first in luxury leather. Instead of integrating the brands he acquires, however, Perrin continues to run them as independent concerns, simply assisting in the spread of expertise.

Growth promoter

Two growth promoters have made Cartier what it is today. Robert Hocq, who sparked off the dynamic forces, lost his life in a tragic road accident in 1979. Since then Alain-Dominique Perrin has headed the administration and marketing of Cartier International.

Hocq's dynamic style was principally that of the coach, but he was also an exploiter. After he had restructured the group he found Perrin, the 'ideas man', who succeeded in marketing the lighters. Hocq took Perrin under his wing and systematically brought him up the profit centre management ladder from product manager to group chief executive.

Perrin continued to exploit the image potential, but more important is his role as the figurehead of the dynamic company. The entire management team is responsible for the company's dynamism, and Perrin's position is supported by everyone's conviction that the best man belongs at the top. To be dynamic a company needs a leader who is both its cement and its dynamite. 'Only a united management which recognizes the qualities of its leader can take a company very far.' Perrin's working style alone is enough to make Cartier dynamic: in spite of the speed with which he makes and acts on decisions he has a detailed knowledge of his company.

Perrin is not afraid to make symbolic gestures. Cartier maintains a staff of detectives and lawyers to protect the brand image by tracking down Cartier imitations anywhere in the world. The fight against forgeries is almost a personal one, culminating in the media spectacle of Perrin himself crushing fake Cartier clocks with a steamroller. He commissioned the artist César to turn some of the resulting scrap metal into pictures, which now hang in his office.

Corporate concept

Cartier's concept is clear and simple. 'The simplest strategies are the best.' The company's overwhelming concern is to control the brand image and protect the brand. The all-important vision of top management means it is entirely market-oriented. The management must be completely familiar with any movements in the market, and must listen to the market as a doctor listens to her patients. It must keep on the move and be everywhere at once. Perrin has succeeded brilliantly in fulfilling the company's aim of taking first place in jewellery, of maintaining and strengthening the power of the name. Now he has other ideas up his sleeve.

Man-management

Perrin's use of motivation at Cartier is excellent. His personal dynamism carries everyone with it.

Executives are promoted up from their own ranks. Management vacancies are always filled internally, regardless of age or other bureaucratic conditions. Perrin himself is a prime example: he was only 26 when Hocq appointed him and other young managers to the management of Cartier.

Time

Speed is not seen as particularly important at Cartier. Products have to be perfect before they are launched. Yet Cartier's timing is masterful. A decision, once taken, is very quickly carried through. When Piaget and Baume & Mercier were acquired, it took only 48 hours to gather all the branch managers in Paris and two days to organize a satellite press conference from Place Vendôme, with journalists simultaneously assembled in Paris, Brussels, Geneva, London, Madrid, Milan and Munich.

Crossair

In 1974 Moritz Suter, then a Swissair DC9 pilot, was asked by some acquaintances to chauffeur them in a hired aircraft. Similar requests followed, with increasing frequency, and in 1975 he and his friend Peter Kalt set up their own flying company, Business Flyers Basel AG, with a share capital of 65,000 SFr.

Their 'fleet' consisted of a twin-engine Cessna and a single-engine Piper, bought secondhand in the summer of 1974. Business Flyers confined itself to hiring out aircraft and occasional pilot training.

Within a few years this 'hobby business', as Suter calls it, had grown into Crossair, a company with a turnover of 133m. SFr. in 1988 and an average annual growth in turnover of 25 per cent. One American newspaper called it 'an economic fairy tale'.

How did the dynamic principle work at Crossair?

Value potential

Regional aviation

Suter's search for value potential was centred on market surveys of regional aviation. The situation was by no means clear, but Suter was convinced that there was sufficient market potential for a regional airline. For example, it was known that 7,000 passengers a year flew from Zurich to Nuremberg via Frankfurt.

Domestic airlines in the USA had shown enormous growth since 1970 and were fast becoming an integral component of the national transport system. Moritz Suter followed American developments with interest: a number of market surveys had shown that regional flight services were needed in Europe too, and so far the major airlines had scarcely noticed the opportunity. In Europe there was much greater competition from road and rail than in the USA, yet even in 1971 surveys had shown that around 80 per cent of business travellers would fly distances of about 600 km.

Suter felt that symbiotic cooperation between national and regional airlines was a very real possibility. Shuttle flights in the regional market niches would bring more passengers to connect with the national airlines, which would in turn increase traffic for the regional companies.

Crossair's success proved him right.

Finances

Crossair has increased its share capital eight times in the last few years: to 1m. in 1978, to 4m. in 1979, to 8m. in 1980, to 16m. in 1981, to 25m. in 1982, to 50m. in 1983, to 80m. in 1985, and finally to 160m. SFr. in 1988. The company was thus able to harness financial potential as well, for it had no problem at all in raising this increased capital. (In 1983 the entire new share issue was taken up by Swiss banks.)

Personnel

Crossair is a small company, and all its employees are directly exposed to Suter's personal dynamism, charisma and determination to succeed, enabling him to harness human potential as well. The feeling of being in a pioneering company and fighting 'all the big boys' is a powerful source of motivation. Working for any aviation company is exciting, and the Crossair family quite evidently enjoy having more direct contact with the business and carrying out a wider variety of duties – from start to finish.

This value potential in the personnel bears fruit not only in high motivation but also in the flexibility of the employees, who are quite willing to carry out every duty there is. This, of course, keeps costs down, and Crossair's pilots happily work for a much lower salary than their colleagues in the larger airlines.

Multiplication

Crossair's success is largely due to Suter's skilful multiplication of the flight network. To begin with, Crossair served only three destinations from Zurich (Nuremberg, Innsbruck and Klagenfurt), but only three years later it was flying to fourteen destinations. Suter recognized the high priority of quickly occupying the strategic routes and airports if he was to establish himself in the European market.

Crossair had to overcome innumerable obstacles in the course of this multiplication. The established airlines were not best pleased to see a young, informal pioneer breaking into the air travel market, and Alitalia in particular was worried that it would suffer losses. Crossair had to engage in protracted negotiations and handle them very imaginatively before it was able to open up some of the more important routes.

Growth promoter

Although Business Flyers blazed no trails, and a second attempt, leasing aircraft, was similarly unspectacular, Moritz Suter did not give up. He could have gone back to his original career as a Swissair pilot, but instead he tried again. His regional airline was a sweeping success, soaring out of the blue to become within ten years the leading regional airline in Europe.

How did Suter do it? Firstly he had an unshakeable determination to 'do something', as demonstrated by his reaction to his first two, disappointing, attempts to set up companies. He simply looked for new value potential with more promise.

Suter as growth promoter was an accelerator, developing the value potential he had found with great commitment. He ensured considerable benefits for all the stakeholders within a short time.

In other words Crossair is another case where all the dynamic principles were applied: a strong-willed growth promoter (Moritz Suter) discovered attractive value potential in running and building up a regional airline, in financing it and in the human field. He also intensively multiplied the process of developing new routes.

Corporate concept

Crossair's corporate concept has contributed greatly to its success. Admittedly it is much less explicit and well-documented than some others, such as Bertelsmann's, but it has featured all the more strongly in the minds of Suter the growth promoter and, soon, of his employees. His vision: 'We will be the largest regional airline in Europe', has been the basis of the dynamics which Crossair evolved. He has concentrated all his energies on turning this vision into reality, stressing speed, a dynamic organizational structure and high motivation.

Structures

Because the company was so small and uncomplicated, every employee had the chance to be widely involved in running it. It had no rigid job structure or institutionalized channels of authority. Every employee could see how he or she was contributing. Everyone was simultaneously a specialist and a generalist. Crossair pilots even served the in-flight coffee themselves.

With work being so varied, challenging and exciting, the company soon had the atmosphere of a family: the Crossair culture grew by itself, without any formal deliberations on corporate identity.

Man-management

Suter's enthusiasm, pleasure and energy infected his employees. He expected a great deal of himself and of them. Lower pay than at Swissair, the obligation to work overtime on Sundays unasked (and unpaid, it says in the contract), cleaning the aircraft in their free time – these are things an established airline could scarcely begin to imagine.

Furthermore Crossair employees have the option to become shareholders in the company, an opportunity taken up by a large part of the workforce.

Time

From its very beginning Crossair has been a very fast-moving company:

Crossair flew its first scheduled flight, to Nuremberg, on 2 July 1979. By 9 July it had concluded cooperation agreements with Swissair. Though remaining independent, the service was integrated into Swissair's international reservation system, and Swissair was to handle the flights. On 1 August Crossair became a member of IATA. In early December it applied to the Bundesamt für Zivilluftfahrt (the Swiss equivalent to the Civil Aviation Authority) for new route concessions to be granted, from Zurich to Turin, Lugano and Lyons, from Basle to Milan and Düsseldorf, and from Berne to Paris. In February it placed the order for aircraft already mentioned. In May the share capital was increased from the existing 4m. to 8m. SFr.

Risk

The risks are considerably reduced by Crossair's cooperation agreements with Swissair. These agreements were concluded when Lufthansa, by arrangement with Swissair, began to fly between Zurich and Hanover and between Zurich and Nuremberg – routes which had previously been Crossair's alone. The contract gives Crossair a firm guarantee of all routes with less than 40 passengers, greatly reducing the competition between Swissair and Crossair. Use of the Swissair reservation system means better use of capacity.

Hanson

The history of Hanson plc goes back to the year 1964, when two British transport companies, Commercial Motors and Oswald Tillotson, were taken over by the Wiles Group. Their Chairman, James Edward Hanson, now Lord Hanson, and Chief Executive Officer, Gordon White, now Sir Gordon, were appointed to the management of the Wiles Group. A year later Hanson was made Chairman. As their existing field of business offered little scope for development, the two men agreed to turn the Wiles Group into an industrial holding company. In 1965 they took over White's family printing and publishing business, Welbecson, and in 1969 the name of the holding company was changed to the Hanson Trust. After the sale of the transport company further acquisitions were made, so that in 1970 the company was active in agricultural products, building materials and equipment, printing and publishing. In 1973, breaking away from the Hanson Trust's exclusively domestic acquisition policy, a group of Hanson managers under the leadership of Gordon White set up an industrial group in the USA, based on the British model, which contributed over 40 per cent to group profits in 1988. Today the company, which is now called Hanson plc, has a total turnover of £7,396m. and includes such well-known firms as Imperial Tobacco, Kaiser Cement, Kidde Inc., Smith Corona Corporation, Allders Limited, London Brick Company and SCM Chemicals in its portfolio.

Value potential

Undermanaged companies

The basic industries in Great Britain in the 1950s and 1960s were contending with a variety of problems. They were unproductive, and their position in international competition was weak. Many companies were family businesses, and even those that were not offered small incentive to new young managers. Companies often had extensive assets, yet, partly because of inflation, their book value was usually way below their market value. Hanson and White exploited this situation by rapidly acquiring a large number of 'undermanaged' companies. Through rigorous restructuring these companies gained value very quickly and could be resold at a profit, either complete or broken up. It was, however, only possible to develop this value potential of 'restructuring undermanaged companies' with highly developed skills in acquisition and restructuring, and innovative forms of financing. The following example will serve as an illustration.

The case of Imperial Tobacco

On 9 December 1985 it was announced in the press that the Hanson Trust had made an offer of £1,900m., from its own resources, for the cigarette and consumer goods producer, the Imperial Group. But Hanson's 'competitive bid' was contested: the Imperial board preferred a rival bid from the food group United Biscuits. Hanson raised the offer to £2,500m. and won the takeover battle.

After the acquisition Hanson drastically reduced administration costs, breaking down the central administration and replacing the centralized top management with a decentralized management with greater responsibility. *The Financial Times* of 5 August 1988 reported that, of 1,060 jobs in Head Office, only 260 remained after restructuring. This division of central management saved £25m. The prestigious administration building in central London was disposed of, and the marketing organization was rationalized so that Imperial Tobacco became a very much fitter, stronger company. Various parts of the company were sold off, to a total value of £2,200m. by 1988.

Multiplication

To Hanson the acquisition of companies is not an extraordinary event but the hub of its business. Hanson consistently multiplies the process of acquisition and restructuring. To achieve smooth multiplication the process is very much standardized. An acquisition and restructuring project runs broadly through the following phases:

- *Evaluation and analysis:* Hanson's interest in a potential candidate for takeover is usually aroused by takeover offers to the shareholders, merger agreements, sales offers or press reports. In a friendly takeover a group of external consultants may possibly undertake an analysis of the candidate's value, cashflow, organizational structure and potential for unbundling.
- *Decision:* If the company meets Hanson's criteria, then the decision is made to acquire it.
- *Purchase/financing:* Hanson was one of the pioneers of 'leveraged buyouts' in the USA. In Britain acquisitions are usually financed by raising external capital in the usual way, or by an exchange of shares.
- *Analysis of the company:* At this stage in a hostile takeover external consultants help to assess the restructuring potential of the target company.
- *Restructuring measures:* As a rule restructuring measures, such as reorganization of management structures or unbundling, are concluded within six months of the acquisition.

By early 1988 this acquisition and restructuring process had been multiplied in 19 transactions and 11 spin-offs in Great Britain, and in 10 transactions with 28 spin-offs in the USA.

Growth promoter

Hanson's extremely successful development has much to do with the personalities of its two founders, Lord Hanson and Sir Gordon White. Lord Hanson comes from a Yorkshire family whose various transport companies were mostly nationalized after the Second World War. He found the British industrial landscape of the 1950s and 1960s largely inefficient and tried to make an active contribution to its recovery, rather than being driven by visions of an industrial empire. In the mid-1960s he saw the enormous potential for increasing value through takeovers and restructuring, and focused on that area.

There is no doubt that Lord Hanson is particularly charismatic. This happy gift, together with great confidence in his employees and the ability to delegate and motivate, has helped him to take Hanson plc up to its current position as the fifth largest company in Great Britain.

Sir Gordon White, a longstanding friend of Lord Hanson's, built up the US side of the Hanson Group, Hanson Industries, in the space of a few years. Tired of British socialism and the power of the unions, Sir Gordon had been looking for fresh fields. He moved to New York in 1973 with $3,000, the maximum that could be taken into the country at that time, and used leveraged buyout financing to build up a concern that by 1988 had a turnover of over $5,400m. Hanson and White make an ideal leadership team: while Sir Gordon is a brilliant negotiating tactician with a marked gift for persuasion, the visionary power is attributed above all to Lord Hanson, whose organizational talents are also pronounced.

Lord Hanson and Sir Gordon White are now over the normal retirement age. It remains to be seen whether the management team they have assembled can continue the dynamic development of the last quarter-century once they have relinquished the reins.

Corporate concept

Although the impression to the casual observer may be that Hanson plc is a complicated and confusing industrial conglomerate, the company actually has a clearly defined concept whose guidelines are consistently applied. For Hanson to make an offer any potential target for acquisition must be:

- Involved in a basic industry
- Not involved with high technology
- Not involved in the service sector
- Well endowed with assets
- Capable of foreseeable cash flow development
- Able to be rapidly restructured.

Most Hanson companies are active in mature and stagnating markets, so that it is possible to estimate with some precision the opportunities and risks of restructuring.

Structures

Flat organizational pyramids

Hanson has a very flat organizational structure. Sir Gordon White, as Chairman, presides over Hanson Industries in the USA, while Lord Hanson, also as Chairman, steers Hanson plc in Great Britain. The direct responsibility for success rests with the second level of management – the directors of the constituent companies. Hanson has only very small staffs at its head offices.

Restructuring aims amongst other things to give Hanson companies flatter organization structures and to transfer operational responsibility to the highest level of management.

Management structure

Hanson gives the individual companies great freedom as far as corporate strategy and functional operations are concerned. The holding company fulfils certain functions centrally: takeovers of firms, cash management and financing, financial supervision of the subsidiaries and strict control of expenditure. The managing directors report weekly, and financial reporting highlights profit before tax and deviations from budget. In contrast to the constant delegation of operational responsibility and authority, financial supervision is tight and inflexible: the managing director of a Hanson subsidiary can, for instance, spend only up to £2,000 over budget.

Man-management

Success is motivating, breeding more success. Nowhere is this more apparent than at Hanson, where every interview revealed pride in the company's achievements. Hanson also motivates its employees by:

- *Extensive delegation of authority.* When Hanson restructures a company, it allows the top executives of any subsidiaries to run their companies without the restrictive interference of the central staff, a liberating experience for many of them.

- *Incentives and financial participation in the company.* The remuneration of a Hanson manager is made up of three components. As well as a basic salary at the going rate he or she receives a bonus in line with the profit on capital invested in the company. The third component is share options in the parent company, Hanson plc. Over 50m. shares have been allocated to the 700 or more top executives in the Group.

- *Direct channels of communication.* Problems are quickly discussed between the parties involved, and the limited hierarchy makes it possible for information to be freely exchanged in all directions.

Time

For a takeover bid to succeed, the bidder must be flexible and react quickly. For example, Hanson managed to raise over $7,000m. in only four days to finance the takeover of Kidde. This ability to act quickly is a result of the flat structures and informal channels of communication referred to above. Hanson is also usually able to limit to six months the period from the first analysis of a target for acquisition until completed restructuring.

Risk

Lord Hanson and Sir Gordon White have shown several times that they are willing to take risks, but they calculate them precisely. The setting of clear objectives and selection of takeover candidates according to strict criteria both reduce risks considerably. The final decision is always made on the basis of an analysis of the 'downside risk'. Their success, then, springs not from gambler's luck, but from pragmatically taking calculated risks.

In conclusion: at Hanson we see the dynamic principle at work again. Two strong growth promoters actively and multiplicatively harness attractive value potential, which they have found in restructuring 'undermanaged' companies.

IKEA

The name IKEA is made up of the initial letters of its founder, Ingvar Kamprad, and his home, a farm called Elmataryd in the village of Agunnaryd in southern Sweden. The company started as a kind of grocery and general store in Småland, and developed in the course of time into a mail order firm. Then, in 1950, Kamprad took over a disused joinery in Älmhult, and in 1953 opened the doors of his first furniture showroom. Four years later he invented self-assembly furniture in handy packs, the idea that was to be the foundation stone of his extraordinary success. Kamprad opened his first furnishing store, with an area of 13,000 square metres, in 1958.

Thirty years on, IKEA has 83 shops in twenty countries, 13,500 employees and an annual turnover of 14,500m. SKr.

IKEA today offers significant benefits to its stakeholders. One of its ruling precepts is this: 'IKEA should offer a wide range of beautiful and functional furniture at affordable prices', and indeed the customers benefit from a range of over 11,000 reasonably priced products from the 'crazy furniture company from Sweden'. IKEA's suppliers all over the world profit from their sales contracts. Last but not least, IKEA's different working style makes it a popular employer.

Value potential

The market for furniture

Kamprad saw the potential for low-priced yet attractive, high-quality, furniture which conventional furniture manufacturers, with their relatively high prices, were not touching. Appreciating the value he could give his customers, he put together a myriad of exciting ideas into the sophisticated network of furniture stores which would harness this potential.

The hallmark of IKEA furniture is simplicity and functionality. Its cheerful Swedish style and bright, youthful colours appeal to people of all ages. Moreover, the company makes high-quality products at low prices. 'We have no respect for a product until we know what it costs.'

IKEA has made good use of all its advantages over the competition. The Swiss furniture industry, for example, believed that taste was very individual, and did not take these egalitarian Swedes seriously. But even the ultra-conservative Swiss customer liked IKEA's low prices and was happy with the new Swedish style of furniture. The IKEA elk revolutionized the market.

One of Kamprad's most important ideas was to reverse the principle of mail order. From the start Kamprad had published a catalogue of his products, and he used to deliver orders on the village dairy's milk lorry, until it changed its route and he had to find a new means of distribution. He found it in the customer. He stopped delivering and got the customers to collect their own furniture from the showroom.

This simple concept really took off when Kamprad began to sell self-assembly furniture in flat packs in 1956. Turnover immediately doubled, to 17m. SKr. The packs saved space and were easy to transport, and this revolutionary idea was to be one of the most important elements of the IKEA system.

Purchasing

Kamprad was looking for new ways of selling furniture at reasonable prices. At first he bought furniture predominantly from Swedish manufacturers, but when they boycotted him he had to find alternative suppliers. Rather than buying ranges of finished furniture, he began to commission furniture to his own specifications, thus harnessing considerable purchasing potential. He placed orders in Denmark, Czechoslovakia, Poland and even Taiwan. The Eastern bloc proved a particularly good source of reasonable suppliers.

Today IKEA is in contact with 1,500 suppliers in forty countries. Half of its supplies come from Scandinavia, and a fifth each from the Eastern bloc and the rest of Europe.

The workforce

The way Kamprad treats his employees bears the stamp of his personality. Working at IKEA is quite different to working in other companies. Kamprad was the first in Sweden to introduce the informal 'du' (for 'you') in business. Everyone addresses everyone else, even the founder, as 'du'. Ties do not have to be worn, and everyone dresses as they feel most comfortable. Freedom is seen as a part of working at IKEA. Similarly no titles are used, and all the employees eat in the staff canteens – there are no directors' dining rooms. The working climate is free from rigid instructions and disciplinary procedures.

For Kamprad it is very important for management not to lose touch with the actual business. It will come as no surprise that he himself often visits the shops to see that everything is all right. There is also a regular roster for all managers right up to the top executives to spend a week working as ordinary warehousemen or salesmen.

Multiplication

IKEA's growth was initially confined to Scandinavia. It was fifteen years after its initial foundation before the first, prototype, furniture store was opened, and the second, which is still the largest store in Stockholm, was not opened until seven years later, in 1965. After that multiplication within Scandinavia was quite rapid, so that by 1972 there were eight branches.

Dynamism really took hold then, as the business was extended to other European countries. Instead of undertaking long, complicated market analyses as a basis for this decision, Kamprad went to Austria for a week and sent his deputy to Switzerland. They carried out personal surveys to try to clarify needs and find the ideal location. Both went home with very clear ideas. They decided on Spreitenbach, near Zurich – if they could gain a foothold in a cautious market like Switzerland, then the rest of Europe would surely be receptive to the IKEA idea. Spreitenbach turned out to be a success, and indeed the rest of Europe was wide open.

Between 1974 and 1984 Kamprad expanded the network to 56 furniture stores in a total of 17 countries. Turnover went up to 6,770m. SKr. In 1988 the 75 branches in 20 countries made a turnover of 14,500 SKr.

Further development cannot yet be predicted. Well over 80 per cent of IKEA's worldwide turnover comes from Europe (57 per cent from Scandinavia and West Germany), and the company does not even have branches yet in all European countries. It has established itself on five continents and the opportunities for further expansion seem to be unlimited. Kamprad is currently even negotiating to build a store in Moscow.

The growth promoter

Ingvar Kamprad is a self-made man with a unique aura. He works with his employees in a simple open-plan office in Aubonne, in the west of Switzerland. His desk is just like all the others, for Kamprad's philosophy is: 'I am, after all, no more than an employee.'

Kamprad is the very personification of the simple life, and believes strongly in austerity. Austerity creates the urge to achieve, and never allows complacency. 'Waste is a mortal sin.' So Kamprad is careful to preserve the austere conditions which are a spur to creativity; for example, he himself drove an old Volvo for years although he could well have afforded a different vehicle altogether.

Ingvar Kamprad resigned from his position at the head of the firm in 1986 and handed over the reins to the young Anders Moberg. Since then he has officially been in retirement, but he is still working and is in charge of product development and purchasing, as well as being a member of the supervisory board.

Corporate concept

Kamprad wove two important ideas into the corporate concept. One is unrestrained energy, pleasure in working and the willingness to take on new challenges. Responsibility goes hand in hand with the admission that anyone can make mistakes. The other idea is his philosophy of simplicity, reflected in an awareness of costs and in the products themselves: 'Throwaway goods and IKEA don't go together. ...But quality must not become an end in itself. It must be suited to the needs of the end user.' Savings are made wherever possible.

'IKEA's own way' is developed from these two basic ideas, as documented in one of their guiding principles: 'Dynamism and a willingness to experiment will always lead us forward. "Why" remains a key word.'

That is probably why IKEA's special system has been so successful, because every one of the furniture stores has an inner harmony. However simple the presentation, there is always an aesthetic note which gives the whole company a very pleasing atmosphere.

Structures

The individual stores are run by national organizations led by a small central management in Denmark. Product and range development are based in Älmhult. Each individual store is a profit centre and has to carry a certain basic range, but is free to stock other goods as well.

Risk

IKEA's development was well planned with every awareness of the risks involved. As already mentioned, it was 1972 before the energetic multiplication of IKEA outside Scandinavia began, and before this a great deal of time had gone into building up the system. In retrospect this careful procedure seems to have been a clever way of limiting the risks.

IKEA relies only on its own financial strength. Its corporate assets belong to a complicated network of IKEA foundations all over the world. All growth is strictly self-financed, which may dampen the growth process but considerably reduces the risks.

Notes

1   Bertelsmann AG, 1985, p. 41.
2   'Wachstumstrategien bei Bertelsmann' (Growth strategies at Bertelsmann), unpublished working paper, p. 10.
3   Bleicher, 1985.

Bibliography

Abell, D. F., *Defining the Business*, Englewood Cliffs 1980.

Abell, D. F., 'Strategic Windows', *Journal of Marketing*, July 1978.

Amato, I., 'Microtool: Small Things Considered', *The Washington Post*, 13 March 1988.

Ansoff, H. I., *Corporate Strategy*, New York 1965.

Argenti, J., *Corporate Collapse – The Causes and Symptoms*, London 1976.

Belz, C., *Konstruktives Marketing*, Savosa/St Gall 1989.

Bennis, W. and Nanus, B., *Leaders*, New York 1985.

Berg, T. L., *Mismarketing – Case Histories of Marketing Misfires*, Garden City 1971.

Bertelsmann AG (ed.), *1835–1985 – 150 Jahre Bertelsmann*, Munich 1985.

Bibeault, D. B., *Corporate Turnaround*, New York 1982.

Biedenkopf, K. H., 'Im Dienst der Gemeinschaft', *150 Jahre Bertelsmann*, Gütersloh 1985.

Bleicher, K., *Chancen für Europas Zukunft*, Frankfurt/Main 1989.

Bleicher, K., 'Führung durch Vorbild', Bertelsmann AG (ed.), *1835–1985 – 150 Jahre Bertelsmann*, Munich 1985.

Borner, S. and Simma, B., 'Unternehmensführung im Strukturwandel', *Die Orientierung*, No. 82, Swiss Volksbank, Berne 1984.

Boyatzis. R. E., *The Competent Manager*, New York 1982.

Bright, D. S., *Gearing up for Fast Lane*, New York 1985.

Buzell, R. D. and Gale, B. T., *The PIMS-Principles*, New York 1987.

Carlzon, J., 'Putting Customer First: The Key to Service Strategy', *The McKinsey Quarterly*, Summer 1987.

Casson, M., 'Recent Trends in International Business: A New Analysis', in Borner, S. (ed.), *International Finance and Trade in a Polycentric World*, Basingstoke, 1988, pp. 215–376.

Cetron, M. J., 'Into the 21st Century: Long-Term Trends Affecting the United States', *The Futurist*, Vol. 22, No. 4, July/August 1988.

Clifford, D. K. and Cavanagh, R. E., *The Winning Performance*, New York 1985.

Deal, T. E. and Kennedy, A. A., *Corporate Cultures*, Reading Mass. 1982.

Drucker, P. F., *Management*, London 1974.

Finneran, K., 'The Future of the English Language', *The Futurist*, Vol. 20, No. 4, July/August 1986.

Foster, R. N., *Innovation*, New York 1986.

Fowles, J., 'Coming Soon: More Men than Women', *The New York Times*, 5 June 1988.

Freudenmann, H., *Planung neuer Produkte*, Stuttgart 1965. Cit. in Siegwart, H., *Produktentwicklung in der industriellen Unternehmung*, Berne 1974.

Goldsmith, W. and Clutterbuck, D., *The Winning Streak*, Harmondsworth 1985.

Greiner, L. E., 'Evolution und Revolution im Wachstum von Organisationen', *Harvard Manager*, No. 3, 1982.

Hamilton, J. O., 'Miracle Drug', *Business Week*, 29 August 1988.

Hanan, M., *Fast Growth Strategies*, New York 1987.

Henderson, B. D., *Die Erfahrungskurve in der Unternehmensstrategie*, Frankfurt/New York 1987.

Hinterhuber, H. H., *Strategische Unternehmensführung*, Berlin/New York 1984.

Hirn, R., 'Warten auf Krieg', *Manager Magazin*, No. 6, 1988.

Höhn, R., *Führungsbrevier der Wirtschaft*, Bad Harzburg 1966.

Hornstein, H. A., *Management Courage*, New York 1986.

Hrebiniak, L. G. and Joyce, W. F., *Implementing Strategy*, New York/London 1984.

Jacobs, K., 'Organizational Renewal: The Jacobs Suchard Experience', *The McKinsey Quarterly*, Winter 1987.

Kirkland, R. I., 'Outsider's Guide to Europe in 1992', *Fortune*, October 24, 1988.

Kirsch, W. and Roventa, P., *Bausteine eines strategischen Managements*, Berlin 1983.

Kobi, J.-M. and Wüthrich, H. A., *Unternehmenskultur verstehen, erfassen und gestalten*, Munich 1986.

Kotter, J. P., *The General Managers*, New York 1982.

Kotter, J. P., *Power and Influence*, New York 1985.

Kouzes, J. M. and Posner, B. Z., *The Leadership Challenge*, San Francisco 1988.

Levitt, T., 'Marketing Myopia', *Harvard Business Review*, July/August 1960.

Levitt, T., 'The Globalization of Markets', *Harvard Business Review*, May/June 1983.

Levitt, T., *The Marketing Imagination*, New York/London 1983.

Leysen, A., 'Krisen sind Herausforderungen', Herford 1986. Cit. in Simon, H., 'Die Zeit als strategischer Erfolgsfaktor', unpublished manuscript, Bielefeld 1988.

Loomis, C. J., 'Buyout Kings', *Fortune*, July 1988.

Lorange, P. and Vancil, R. F., 'How to Design a Strategic Planning System', *Harvard Business Review*, September/October 1976.

Lorange, P., *Strategic Planning Systems*, Englewood Cliffs 1977.

Love, J. F., *McDonald's – Behind the Arches*, New York 1986.

Maccoby, M., 'Self-Developers: Why the Engineers Work', *IEEE Spectrum*, Vol. 26, No. 2, February 1988.

Management Enzyklopädie, 2nd ed., Landsberg/Lech 1983.

Mayo, J. S., 'New Developments in Computer and Communications Technologies', *Vital Speeches of the Day*, Vol. 53, No. 16, 1 June 1987.

Meffert, H., 'Größere Flexibilität als Unternehmenskonzept', *Zeitschrift für Betriebswirtschaft*, No. 37, 2/1985.

Meffert, H., *Marketing*, 3rd ed., Wiesbaden 1977.

Merriam, J. E. and Makover, J., *Trend Watching*, New York 1988.

Mills, D. Q., *The New Competitors*, New York 1985.

Mohn, R., *Erfolg durch Partnerschaft*, Berlin 1986.

Moser, P., 'The McDonald's mystique', *Fortune*, 4 July 1988, pp. 112–116.

Moss-Kanter, R., *The Change Masters*, New York 1983.

Myers, N., 'Writing off the Environment', *Green Pages: The Business of Saving the World*, Routledge 1988.

Naisbitt, J., *Megatrends*, London/Sydney 1984.

Nayak, P. R. and Ketteringham, J. M., *Breakthroughs*, New York 1986; London 1987.

Ohmae, K., *Triad Power*, New York 1985.

Percy, C. H. and McMinn, D. W., 'The World's Biggest Market. How Companies Can Keep Europe Open', *The New York Times*, 9 October 1988.

Peters, T. J. and Waterman, R. H., *In Search of Excellence*, New York 1982.

Peters, T. J., *Thriving on Chaos*, New York 1985.

Pleitner, H. J., 'Entrepreneurs and New Venture Creation: Some Reflections of a Conceptual Nature', *Journal of Small Business & Entrepreneurship*, Vol. 4, Summer 1986.

Porter, M. E., *Competitive Advantage*, New York 1985.

Porter, M. E., 'Competitive Advantage of Nations', unpublished working paper, Boston 1988.

Porter, M. E., *Competitive Strategy*, New York 1980.

Porter, M. E., 'From Competitive Advantage to Corporate Strategy', *Harvard Business Review*, May/June 1987.

Probst, G. J. B., *Kybernetische Gesetzeshypothesen als Basis für Gestaltungs- und Lenkungsregeln im Management*, Berne 1981.

Pümpin, C., 'The Practice of Strategic Management', *The Orientation*, Swiss Volksbank, Berne 1981a.

Pümpin, C., 'Building Strategic Success Potential: A Central Corporate Mission', in Wittmann, W. (ed.), *Free Enterprise – Pillar of the Future*, Stuttgart 1981b.

Pümpin, C., 'Unternehmenskultur, Unternehmensstrategie und Unternehmenserfolg', in *Die Bedeutung der Unternehmenskultur für den zukünftigen Erfolg Ihres Unternehmens*, Allgemeine Treuhand AG (ATAG), Basle 1984.

Pümpin, C., 'La culture de l'entreprise: Le Profil Stratégique qui conduit au succès', *L'information*, No. 85, Swiss Volksbank, Berne 1985.

Pümpin, C. and Echevarría, G., *Cultura Empresarial*, Ediciones Díaz de Santos, Madrid 1988.

Pümpin, C., *The Essence of Corporate Strategy*, Gower Publishing, Aldershot 1989.

Quinn, J. B., 'Innovationsmanagement: Das kontrollierte Chaos', *Harvard Manager*, No. 4, 1985.

Ramirez, A., 'Making Better Use of Older Workers', *Fortune*, 30 January 1989.

Rappaport, A., *Creating Shareholder Value*, New York 1986.

Ries, A. and Trout, J., *Positioning: The Battle for Your Mind*, New York 1986.

Robertson, A. B., Achilladelis, B. and Jervis, B., *Success and Failure in Industrial Innovation*, Report on Project Sappho, London 1972.

Schelker, T., 'Problemlösungsmethoden im Produktinnovationsprozeß', Dissertation, St Gall 1976.

Siegwart, H., Caytas, I. G. and Mahari, J. I., 'Financial Design setzt Energien frei', *Harvard Manager*, No. 1, 1988a.

Siegwart, H., Caytas, I. G. and Mahari, J. I., 'Turnaround Management: von quantitativen zu qualitativen Sanierungsstrategien', *Der Schweizer Treuhänder*, Special Edition III 1–2, 1988b.

Simon, H., 'Die Zeit als strategischer Erfolgsfaktor', unpublished manuscript, Bielefeld 1988.

Suplee, C., 'Computer Design: Is This Machine Thinking or Not?', *Washington Post*, 5 October 1986.

Tapie, B., *Gagner*, Paris 1986.

Tichy, N. M. and Devanna, M. A., *The Transformational Leader*, New York 1986.

Turner, G., 'The Future Ambitions of Japan's Financial Giants', *Long Range Planning*, Vol. 20, No. 5, October 1987.

Ulrich, H., *Die Unternehmung als produktives soziales System*, 2nd ed., Berne 1970.

Ulrich, H., *Unternehmenspolitik*, 2nd ed., Berne 1987.

Vancil, R. F. and Lorange, P., 'Strategic Planning in Diversified Companies', *Harvard Business Review*, January/February 1975.

Wall Street Journal, 'Glutted Markets: A Global Overcapacity Hurts Many Industries. No Easy Cure is Seen', 9 March 1987.

Wehrli, H. P., 'Marketing – Zürcher Ansatz', Dissertation, Zurich 1980.

Weinhold, H., *Marketing in 20 Lektionen*, 16th ed., St Gall/Stuttgart/Steyr 1988.

Whitney, J. O., 'Turnaround Management Every Day', *Harvard Business Review*, September/October 1987.

Winteler, H., 'Strukturwandel des Goldmarktes', *Neue Zürcher Zeitung*, 20 December 1988.

de Woot, P., *Management Stratégique des Groupes Industriels*, Paris 1984.

Wunderer, R. and Grunwald, W., *Führungslehre*, Vol. 1, Berlin 1980.

Index